Sunset
Ideas for Planning
YOUR NEW HOME

By the Editors of Sunset Magazine
and Sunset Books

Lane Publishing Co. · Menlo Park, California

THE HOUSE ON THE COVER is a provocative example of what can be done with the use of sky-lights. Glass walls open the house to the out-of-doors and the unusual skylight system opens the roof over every room. Architect: Jacob Robbins. See page 96.

Edited by Sherry Gellner

Editor, Sunset Books: David E. Clark

Fifteenth Printing October 1977

Contents

Your most important investment...

For the great majority of homeowners, the most important single investment of their lifetime is the house they live in. With this in mind, we have tried to make this book *not* just another collection of room schemes, but a carefully edited selection of fresh ideas, tried-and-true plans, and custom touches. It is hoped that the work of the many fine architects and designers represented in these pages will heighten the reader's understanding of sound planning principles.

All of the houses in this book have been reported in recent issues of *Sunset Magazine*. Several of them were award winners in the Western Home Awards program, a continuing review of residential house designs in the thirteen Western states jointly sponsored by the American Institute of Architects and *Sunset Magazine*.

HOW THIS BOOK IS ORGANIZED

This book is divided into six chapters. There's a chapter each for houses in the following five categories: Single-level houses; multi-level houses; small houses for small lots; houses for the country, mountains, and seashore; and houses for the desert. The houses shown in each chapter were carefully selected to appeal to a wide variety of tastes and living habits—from roomy or expandable houses geared to a growing family, to more modest structures suited to a retired couple. The sixth chapter is a potpourri of ideas for making the interior of your house more comfortable and livable.

When you first thumb through this book, you may not sense the pervading element that welds these six chapters into a logical whole. However, upon further study, you will find that the design of every house or idea included in the book reflects the way daily living can be met with freshness and vigor.

In this book you will see the skillful, natural way some houses meet and merge with the out-of-doors—how others are built to frame a view.

You will see open planning tailored to create space and an atmosphere of unhampered movement. And you will find examples of how new materials and devices have been employed to give more house for the building dollar.

WHAT TO LOOK FOR IN A FLOOR PLAN

Were you to study only the floor plans in this book, without looking at a single photograph, you would discover that many houses, though differing in detail, have significant features in common.

Planned to the lot line: A great many of the houses are designed to take full advantage of their climate to permit maximum outdoor living. In some areas outdoor space is just as important as the indoors; hence, many of the plans show architectural thinking clear to the lot line.

Placement of the house on the lot is conceived as only one problem in the total use of available space. If there are fences, these become in one sense the true walls of the house. With or without boundary fencing, many plans provide for outlook beyond the lot line, to gain maximum visual space. Circulation through the house and garden is planned as a single traffic pattern.

Look at the compass points on the plans. You will see how the designers have oriented these houses to take advantage of the sun's benign influence and to avoid its punishing effects. The houses located in cool, coastal areas where solar heat is needed, have window walls faced to catch the sun. In hot inland locations, the house plan may open to the east or north and turn a blind, windowless wall to the west. Where wind is bothersome, control is often established with fencing, planting, and carefully located windows and exterior doors.

Indoor-outdoor relationship: In the full use of the total available space, these plans show a close linkage between indoor and outdoor space. Patio, terrace, and deck are treated as an extension of living space. The outdoor room may adjoin a bedroom, living room, kitchen, dining room, or an all-purpose room, enhancing the livability of the indoor room.

Indoors, outdoors merge

ARCHITECTS: CAMPBELL AND WONG

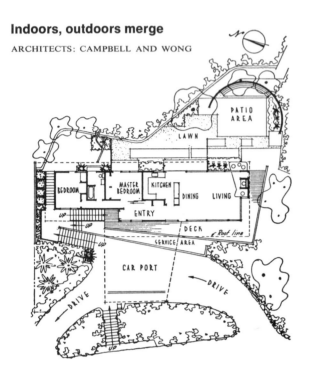

Many of the plans have two or more patios or decks, usually designed for differing functions. One may be related to the living area, one to the bedroom wing; one exposed for summer sun, the other enclosed for winter use; one for children, another for adults; or one for family hobbies and another for formal entertaining.

Open planning: A very important feature of good house design is open planning, applied principally to the entertaining-cooking-dining area of the house. In builders' houses, this feature is often included to save on construction costs; but in the collection of houses in this book, open planning is included for its own value. The open plan fits the informal, servantless ways of today's living; and it provides the feeling of space in a compact house.

The floor plans provide for the free circulation of family and guests, so the closely related activities of cooking, eating, and entertaining may be enjoyed without tiresome detours. Some plans show no doors between kitchen and dining areas, some

omit walls, some provide movable walls (sliding panels, folding doors, removable screens) so the area can be opened up or boxed in, as circumstances dictate. Alcoves and high counters conceal kitchen clutter from the dinner guests.

Although closed planning is still the rule in most of the sleeping-bathing areas shown in this book, even here you will notice plans that bring some of the benefits of open planning to this normally compartmented area. Privacy without absolute enclosure is provided by balcony bedrooms, elevated above eye level; by sliding doors, screens, or curtains; or by glass walls that open to the outdoors. Even that ultimate refuge, the bathroom, participates discreetly in open planning through small adjoining patios, garden airwells, or clerestory windows that let in the sky and the tree tops.

Zoned for livability: All of the plans in this book separate interior space into zones of activity. Most of the plans recognize two major zones, one an active area devoted to entertaining, dining, and cooking, and the other a zone for quiet and privacy where bedrooms and bathrooms are located.

The pavilion arrangement: This arrangement goes one step farther in planning for zoned living: It provides for separate buildings, each with its own roof and four walls. All buildings are linked

A four-pavilion complex

ARCHITECTS: MARQUIS AND STOLLER

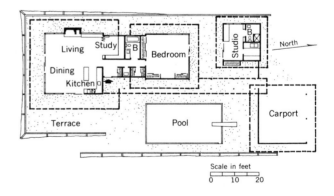

together by roofed-over galleries, outdoor passageways, or enclosed decks. Each building has a separate function—a sitting room retreat for the adults; an area where young people can entertain their friends or where youthful projects can be pursued; an area for isolating the laundry, service, or workshop activities.

(See coverage of this house on page 16)

SINGLE-LEVEL HOUSES

A house entirely on one level makes particularly good sense for young married couples, families with small children, and persons of retirement age. Generally speaking, the building-cost-per-square-foot is quite reasonable. Also, the house without stairways is easier and safer for the very young child and for the elderly or infirm person.

Before purchasing a single-level house, be sure to give careful consideration to the possibilities for future expansion. Many young couples settle in the house of their dreams, putting all of their energies and love into it, only to find later that space is short for a growing family and there is no way to expand. Assuming your lot will permit an addition, it is usually architecturally easier and less expensive to provide for expansion in a single-level house than in one with multiple levels.

Possibly your only desire is to have a house where the outdoors can be enjoyed as much as the indoors—where you can have a living room opening on the same level as a garden or expanse of lawn, a bedroom looking out on a grove of trees, a kitchen with a window above the sink rather than a wall or cupboard. Note how many of the houses shown in this chapter combine indoor living with the out-of-doors.

CONCRETE WALL *at right is 5½ inches thick, has interesting surface texture with rocks hand-placed when slab was formed. It was poured at the site—tilted upward to vertical position; surface inside house similar.*

Skylight gives daylit quality

ARCHITECT: TED BOWER

DIVIDER *screens the kitchen. Bamboo curtains in background conceal range, refrigerator, work counter, storage. Shelf across top is for display.*

A plastic skylight, raised above ceiling height and sweeping the full length of the living room and beyond, gives this house a spacious daylit quality. Yet it's a small house of only 1,430 square feet.

Two other interesting features are the tilt-up concrete wall (shown in the photo above), and the way the master bedroom can be made a part of the living room (see floor plan). This is a convenient arrangement as it means that the fire can be enjoyed from the bedroom as well as from the kitchen-living-dining areas.

The house has other special qualities about it having been built entirely by the owners over a six-year period. The owner, who was already a hobby carpenter, developed into a better-than-average cabinet maker (he made more than a hundred drawers).

PLASTIC SKYLIGHT, *raised 16 inches above ceiling height, gives the living area a light, spacious feeling. The master bedroom in rear can be part of living area as shown here, or be closed off by folding doors.*

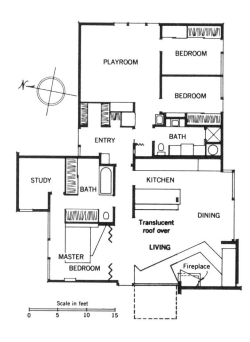

PLAYROOM

BEDROOM

BEDROOM

ENTRY

BATH

STUDY

BATH

KITCHEN

DINING

Translucent roof over

MASTER BEDROOM

LIVING

Fireplace

Scale in feet
0   5   10   15

ENTRY HALL *separates the adult bedroom, bath, and study from the children's bedrooms and playroom.*

WINDOW *frames sunsets in winter, is shaded from summer sun by skylight extending beyond house wall.*

FROM THE STREET, *house has a simple, private facade. Note large paved area for off-street guest parking at left, in front of the privacy fence. Planting area between entry walk and carport parking is skylit.*

House and site planned as one

ARCHITECT: ROBERT BILLSBROUGH PRICE

This house was considered as just one element in the total site plan. From nearly all its rooms, you can see or enter a paved or planted outdoor area screened for privacy.

Note how smoothly these indoor and outdoor areas work together. The dining room has a matching terrace. Off the family room is a living terrace close to the house, leading to another pergola-sheltered area at the rear. Next to the living room is an area of terrace and planting. Off the bedrooms is a play terrace. And the master bedroom opens to a terrace at one end of the rear area.

The interior divides into a large open area for living activities on one side, a sleeping wing on the other. The street face of the house is blank, but callers at the entry can be seen from the kitchen through an open-work fence.

LOOKING FROM GARDEN SHELTER *toward rear of house, left to right: bedrooms, living and family room.*

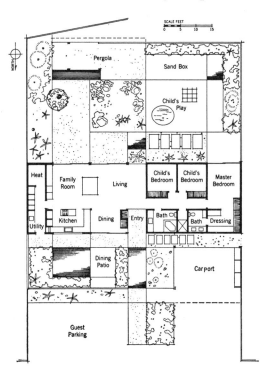

Cool in summer, snug in winter

ARCHITECTS: WALKER AND McGOUGH

Situated in a region of extreme temperatures, summer and winter, this house responds year-around to its environment. Wide roof overhangs above doors and windows encourage the family to move outdoors when it's pleasant, cool the skylit interiors in summer by excluding direct sun, and hold winter weather at arm's length. Inside, the living room serves as a kind of formal buffer between the informal activity area and the bedroom area.

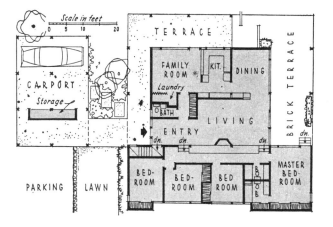

HIGH-BRANCHING TREES *are backdrop for clean lines of house. Roof of double carport extends to the entry walk.*

FAMILY ROOM *has plastic-laminate-topped cabinet for storage of children's toys; this is view from kitchen.*

SKYLIGHTS POUR DAYLIGHT *into living room. Note high ceiling effect; high overhang shelters but allows view.*

HELICOPTER PHOTOGRAPH *shows four separate buildings linked by roofed-over, glass-enclosed galleries. A central patio is paved and planted, surrounded by four pavilions. Pathways lead to garden, around house.*

Pavilion plan...for "zoned living"

ARCHITECT: HENRIK BULL   "DISCOVERY HOUSE" SPONSORED BY SUNSET MAGAZINE

The helicopter photograph of this house (shown above) readily explains the pavilion arrangement of its floor plan. Four separate buildings are linked by roofed-over, glass-enclosed galleries, or outdoor passageways. Each of these "living zones" has a separate function. The Discovery House was originally planned and sponsored by *Sunset Magazine* and the architect as an idea laboratory for people who are in the house-dreaming, house-planning, or house-shopping stage.

The house plan provides each family member with his own private domain, yet also supplies places for the family to be together. Parents have a sitting room retreat for themselves or for intimate entertaining, opening off their bedroom. Each child has a room of his own and they share a common recreation area.

One of the pavilions is for all the family. It has the entry, the living and dining areas, and the kitchen. Isolated in the service pavilion are such noisy activities as laundry, repair work, and shop or craft projects that are best kept away from other living areas.

The enclosed central court is the largest room of the house, with floor and walls, but open to the sky. The patio's walls are the solid redwood walls of the house.

Only the parents' pavilion has windows on the patio and these are curtained.

The striking aspect of the family pavilion is that it puts living, dining, kitchen, and entry into 676 square feet without seeming cramped. Within the main living area, an L-shaped partition creates two sides of the sitting area. An opposite L-shaped section of bare floor directs foot traffic around the seating arrangement and also sets off the dining area. The kitchen is open to the living area by means of a see-through, pass-through wall of shelves. When guests are being entertained, tall shutters can conceal the kitchen from view.

Of all the pavilions in this house, the master bedroom-sitting room has the most luxurious sense of space. It has a fireplace, terrace, and accordion, stow-away partition. The folding partition is nine feet high. Drawn part way, it screens off the bed from the sitting area without destroying the effect of the 24-foot room length and glass wall.

The arrangement of walls and openings in the children's pavilion helps to make the rooms seem much more spacious. Windows are only at one end, a door and closet at the other.

AT ENTRY GATE *your attention is drawn to pool and fountain as a focal point, then to the tall front door.*

MAIN SITTING AREA *contains leather-upholstered sofas that seat 6 people generously; dining area in foreground.*

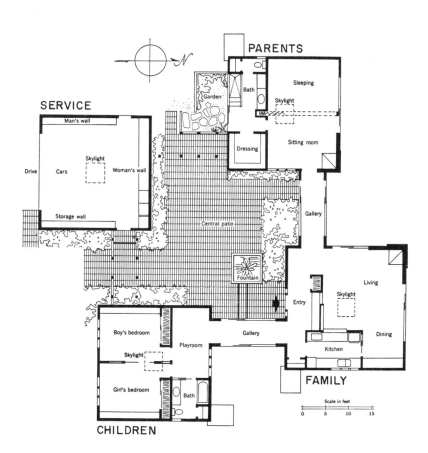

FOOT TRAFFIC *goes through the only hallway needed for through passage in the family pavilion. Using it, you can move from parents' to children's pavilions without entering the living area.*

(Continued on next page)

SITTING ROOM *side of large room in parents' pavilion, seen from bedroom side. Folding partition divides room.*

GIRL'S ROOM, *seen from boy's room through open sliding panels between rooms; counter is used for desk.*

CORRIDOR-TYPE KITCHEN *is compact for step-saving. Large windows over sink counter look out on garden.*

AMPLE STORAGE *in service pavilion includes two laundry bins and a laundry cart built in under counter.*

Four pavilions astride a hilltop

ARCHITECTS: MARQUIS & STOLLER

The floor plan for this four-pavilion complex is informal. One pavilion contains the living areas, one the master sleeping-and-bath facilities. One is a studio-guest pavilion. The fourth is for cars. The pavilions are not the same size, nor are they arranged symmetrically. The house was an award winner in an A.I.A.-Sunset Western Home Awards program.

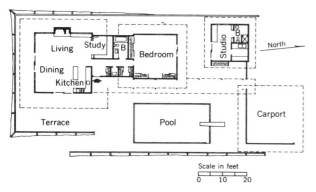

DOTTED LINES *indicate roof lines of the pavilions and the covered entry walk. Pool is part of the entry.*

THE VIEW *on one side is of high mountain with its unspoiled slopes. Garden is just the native brush.*

Two pavilions on a hillside deck

ARCHITECT: JACOB ROBBINS

Here we have a house that neatly provides a four-way separation of activities: sleeping in the north wing, living in the south wing; children to the east, parents to the west. A glass-enclosed gallery links the two wings. A generous deck affords level outdoor living despite the steep slope. The house was an award winner in an A.I.A.-Sunset Western Home Awards program.

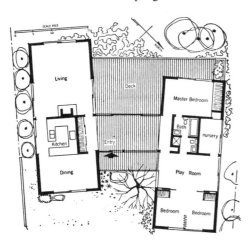

TWO-HOUSE PLAN *is linked together by glass gallery and generous deck. Gallery handles all foot traffic.*

FROM SLOPE BELOW, *house looks like two houses through eucalyptus. Sleeping wing at left; living at right.*

OUTDOOR LIVING AREA *is paved terrace off family room; heating coil in paving helps "extend" summer.*

Indoor-outdoor living on a wooded lot

ARCHITECTS: KIRK, WALLACE, McKINLEY & ASSOC.

THREE TERRACES, *each terminated by a bench, are joined by bridges.*

For their wooded and sloping lot in Vancouver, Washington, the owners wanted a house that would open out to the trees and the view southwest across the Columbia River. They wanted, at the same time, to shut themselves off from the street. (For exterior view see page 7.)

The architects designed and placed the house so that only four of the existing trees had to be removed. On the garden side they used a great deal of glass, and the living and sleeping areas of the house all look out on this side.

On the street side, a long brick wall runs across the width of the lot, opening only for the driveway. Light is brought in by a clerestory in the living room and by narrow, high windows in other parts of the house.

LIVING ROOM *ceiling is raised above main ridge beam; clerestory windows pull in light from street side.*

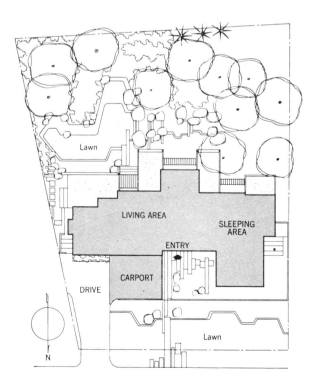

U-SHAPED KITCHEN *has valance lighting on all walls.*

LIVING ROOM *faces rear garden to north. Fireplace set in glass wall provides focal point for orienting furniture. Foot traffic goes along far wall, from entry to doors to dining room and to terrace.*

A garden for every room

ARCHITECTS: CRILEY AND McDOWELL

An outdoor area matches every room in this house except the children's bathroom. Living room, dining room, and family room open to the rear terrace and garden by means of doors in a glass wall; the view the glass offers is also shared by the kitchen. The master bedroom has a fenced-in deck and a bathroom garden; both are private.

The house takes the shape of a cross, with the kitchen at the crux. The living zone (living room, kitchen, and family room) is surmounted by a large gable. A flat roof covers the sleeping zone on the street side, and the dining room. The intersection of the flat roof and gable provides clerestory windows to light the interior kitchen.

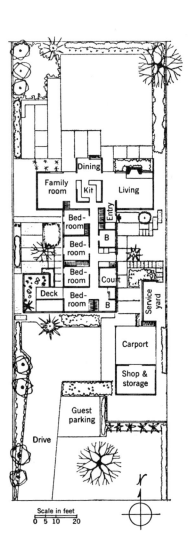

HOUSE IS PRIVATE *from the street; has large paved car-maneuvering area, off-street parking (right). Workshop and planting conceal the carport.*

SHUTTER DOORS *can be opened or closed and guests can be directed to the entry hall or into the lanai (straight ahead over pool). Court and lanai can be used separately, or opened up as one for parties.*

Entry court and lanai serve as "buffer"

ARCHITECT: JOHN TATOM

A definite feeling of shelter was created by building this house around a central court and lanai. The court and lanai (see plan) function as a buffer between a living-dining-kitchen wing and a sleeping wing.

The rather massive, almost adobe-like quality of the house, is achieved by using plaster inside and out; the exterior walls have a rough, hand-trowelled finish. Door and window frames are built out 16 inches to give the walls a sculptural sense of depth—actually they're only 2 inches thick.

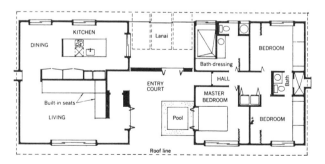

SLEEPING QUARTERS *at right have louvered bi-fold doors on bedrooms for ventilation; draperies conceal closets.*

DIVIDER *serves as display shelf for plants, art objects. Skylight above serves living and dining rooms.*

ROOF SHAPE *of house makes it possible to have high windows for balanced daylight without sacrificing privacy. Living area (left), sleeping area (right) are linked by roof over the carport and entry.*

Organized into two clearly separate

ARCHITECT: ROGER LEE

Nestled on a tree-studded slope, this house is organized into two clearly separated areas—one for living and one for sleeping. A central hall makes it possible to move easily and directly from the entry to any of the rooms. An outdoor route for moving between rooms is provided by a deck that begins in front and ends at the rear at the upper level of the lot.

The deck, with its solid rail, and the street-side face of the house, almost blank except for high windows, com-bine to give the house privacy from the street without blocking the view. The living-dining-kitchen area of the house looks out at the view of the mountains, but is partly open and partly under louvered shade. This whole area is conveniently handy to the kitchen.

The area in the upper right hand corner of the floor plan provides for a later addition of a bedroom. It would also take hall space from the study adding a gallery hall and creating a court.

STARTING AT STREET SIDE, *deck is floor-level outdoor area around half of house. Solid rail provides privacy.*

STREET FACADE, *private except for living room windows above the deck rail, shows how house nestles on slope.*

AFTER DARK, *lights guide you directly to entry from carport. Translucent screen conceals the service yard.*

STUDY *is equipped for guest sleeping. It looks out on rear garden; gets added light from clerestory windows.*

areas, for living and sleeping

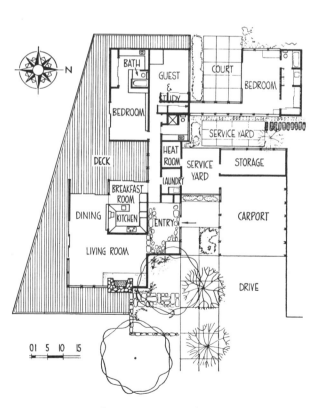

CENTRAL HALL *places rooms at ends of foot traffic paths, free of through traffic. Deck provides outdoor route.*

IN LIVING ROOM, *dropped ceiling over sitting area has sheltering effect to contrast with open space beyond.*

SLIDING WALL PANEL, *louvered shutters can close off the living room on each side from the gardens.*

Open to gardens

ARCHITECT: FRANK SLAVSKY

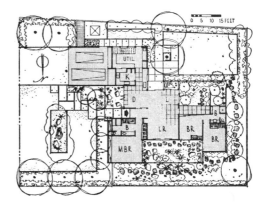

Sliding wall panels or louvered shutters can open the rooms of this house or close them off from the weather. Even when closed, rooms are well ventilated. On a subdivision lot with no view, the house is private from the street and close neighbors, but not forbidding. Its entry promises beauty within; its inner garden world fulfills the promise.

In Hawaii, this house makes sense with its open design and provision for ventilation. On the mainland, where your house can't be completely open, you can use its basic idea if you add glass and heating.

ENTRY *door in facade is of grille and translucent plastic. The screening at the left of entry gives privacy to dining room garden.*

FOLDING SHUTTERS *lead to bedroom garden, provide ventilation.*

VIEW FROM ENTRY *looks toward fireplace and garden beyond. Hearth also provides ample seating space.*

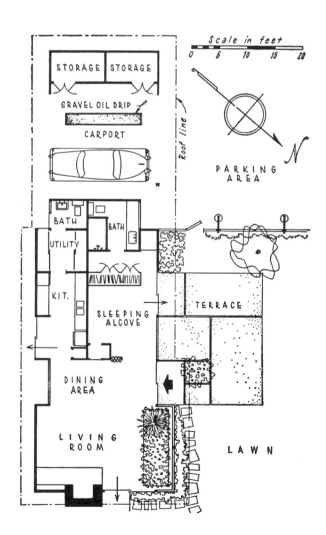

Small but roomy

ARCHITECTS: HOWELL AND ARENDT

Small and informal, this "house for retirement" is made up of areas rather than rooms—for living-dining, cooking, sleeping. Only a folding accordion door separates the sleeping alcove from the living room, and there is no door between living room and kitchen. Although this design makes no special provision for overnight guests, it would be easy enough to add minimum sleeping quarters to the carport storage area by widening it only slightly.

The whole house has the pleasant airy feeling of a summer house, open to garden views, light, and sun.

SMALL AND INFORMAL, *the house opens to paved patio, wide expanse of lawn. Screen of tall trees in background.*

A central court in a simple rectangle

ARCHITECT: JOHN L. FIELD

In an ingeniously simple way, this house reconciles the owners' desires for a view, sun control, and privacy from near neighbors. It is a rectangular design, with a sky-light-roofed central court or atrium. It has blank walls front and back (east and west sides). Each room has a glass wall (on the north and south sides). The house was an award winner in an A.I.A.-Sunset Western Home Awards program.

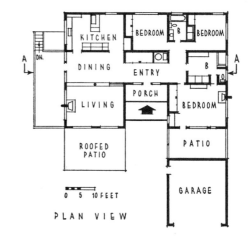

ATRIUM acts as central hall, with access to all rooms. Spotlights above skylight light the area at night.

High, white ceilings give spacious effect

DESIGNER: KIPP STEWART

The architect of this house made the most of the qualities of white, unbroken plaster areas to increase the apparent size of rooms. The rooms were already opened with a soaring, sloping ceiling above the only partition. High windows set in gable peaks further increased this spacious effect. Changes in level, of the ceiling over the entry and of the living room floor, provide a pleasing contrast of space and help define the limits of open areas.

PLAN VIEW

HIGH PORTHOLES in ceiling help to light living room; white plaster ceiling adds to expansive feeling.

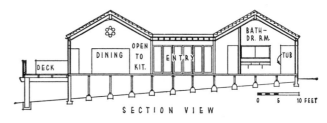

SECTION VIEW

Modern adobe...cool and spacious

DESIGNER: PETER EDWARDS

Adobe and redwood, the principal materials of this ranch type house blend happily with one another and with the outdoors, to which the interior is linked by ample glass openings.

Its floor is at ground level, continuously surfaced (with patio tile) indoors and out. Changes in floor level and roof line accommodate it to the contours of its sloping site. On the uphill side it opens to patio, garden, and play yard, with shade for hot summer days.

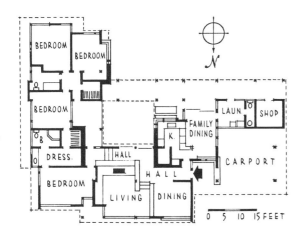

BOOKSHELVES *and low adobe wall separate dining hall from living room. Note living room's lower level.*

Stones in concrete

ARCHITECT: THOMAS O. WELLS

This informal house embraces the slope of the hill on its ranch site in Hawaii. Although it is quite appropriate for this setting, it could be equally at home on the right site on the mainland.

It's a small house (1,100 square feet) that uses the large stones-exposed-in-concrete technique. Stone was collected on the site. The need for specialized labor was eliminated with the use of formed masonry rather than laid-up masonry. The wood timbers were precut. The house was an award winner in an A.I.A.-Sunset Western Home Awards program.

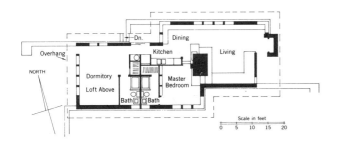

LOW MASONRY WALLS *continue beyond house to embrace the slope. Wood timbers for house were precut.*

Two neighboring U-plan houses...

ARCHITECTS: KILLINGSWORTH, BRADY, SMITH AND ASSOC.

The two houses shown on this page were designed as neighbors in a group of three houses. Both share a form of U-shaped floor plan. In both you enter on a walkway across a pool. Both use wood in an interesting, tailored way. Note how the dramatic entry court of the house to the left separates the bedroom wings from one another.

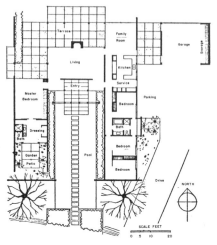

ENTRANCE *is a walkway across water garden in a court between bedroom wings. House is private from street, entry, opens to view on other side.*

...each has an entry walk across water

The house to the right has a similarly-shaped floor plan except that the court is divided into two areas. One of these, at the core of the house, is intimate in feeling and serves as an outdoor living area. The larger court serves the living room and master bedroom.

Both houses were award winners in an A.I.A.-Sunset Western Home Awards program.

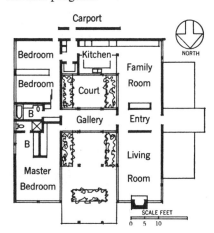

VIEW OF HOUSE *is from entry of house shown at top of page. Its height (9 feet above the street) provides some privacy for side facing view.*

(*See coverage of this house on page 36*)

MULTI-LEVEL HOUSES

Resurging in popularity during recent years—mainly due to increasing demands for larger houses—the multi-level house can give added square footage for a growing family without sacrificing outdoor space.

Often a house built on different levels will be the direct result of a desire to have living and sleeping areas distinctly removed from each other. Of course, another appealing factor to a busy housewife is upkeep, since rooms on another level do not have to be in perfect order at all times.

A house that lifts you upward will often provide a view that would otherwise be cut off at ground level. A deck on the upper level can serve as an outdoor room where you can enjoy the view at your leisure.

The multi-level house is usually the best answer for preserving the natural beauty of a heavily wooded lot. At times, the *only* solution is to build straight up—to blend with the tall trees and add to the measure of privacy. Often, a sloping lot will permit a structure to rise in graduating heights—just as a stairway has one step above another. Either way, with the use of clerestory windows or two-story window walls, you can enjoy the outdoors from within. In this chapter, note the many building techniques used to preserve the natural endowments of the land.

DAYLIGHT PENETRATES *high-ceilinged upper level hall through row of windows (at upper right); windows are continued around end of house. Tall trees screen house from neighbors, add to view from inside.*

It makes the most of natural light

ARCHITECT: A. O. BUMGARDNER AND PARTNERS

In many ways this house makes the most of natural light. Clerestories, window walls, and a lightwell bring daylight inside the house, and glass above the bedroom doors and over wardrobes admits light from interior spaces nearby.

The photographs show the detailing of the interior and how successfully the light does move about inside the house. The sketches on the opposite page explain how this is accomplished.

An upper hall is the unifying central spine of the house. It uses space luxuriously, and is the means the architects used to pull daylight through the ends of the house. Of particular interest is the way light is pulled into the hall over a dressing room and wardrobe (see the sketch on the far right).

The lightwell in the sketch on the left has a double

function. It lets light filter down to the kitchen level and reveals the floor below.

The main outdoor living area is a deck that runs along the sunny south and west sides of the house (see floor plan opposite). Unlike the solid upper hall railing, the railing around the deck is open. However, the spaces between the vertical supports are covered with an unclimbable wire mesh that doesn't afford a toehold for small children.

The house was set in a grove of madrona trees in such a way that only a few trees had to be removed. The trees screen the house from its neighbors and add leafy interest to the views through the high glass. The roof dips low toward the parking area at the front to make a covered loggia for stormy days, partly concealing an entry garden and giving it a greater element of surprise.

WARDROBE *is at end of hall beyond the lightwell. On opposite side is dressing room. Note stairwell at left.*

SMALL, CURIOUS ONLOOKERS *are protected from falling by 33-inch-high solid railing. Good light from above.*

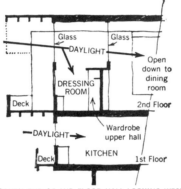

SECTION THROUGH LIVING ROOM LOOKING SOUTH

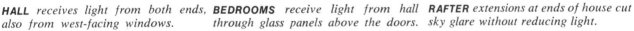

SOUTH END OF 2ND FLOOR HALL LOOKING WEST

SECTION THROUGH BEDROOM

HALL *receives light from both ends, also from west-facing windows.*

BEDROOMS *receive light from hall through glass panels above the doors.*

RAFTER *extensions at ends of house cut sky glare without reducing light.*

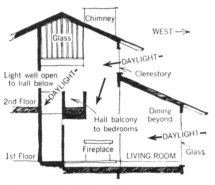

MAIN FLOOR   UPPER FLOOR

THREE LEVELS *make up the house if you count the basement. Living room is two steps lower than dining room.*

ENTRY HALL *has a glass wall for viewing sunken garden and also a glass front door. The studio is opposite.*

EXTERIOR SIDING *is rough-sawn cedar. Brick driveway was installed by owners, helping to cut costs.*

Building costs kept to a minimum

ARCHITECTS: ANDERSON AND BELL

EXTENSION OF BALUSTERS *forms a telephone alcove. Architects designed door screen to go with obscure glass.*

From the beginning the owners of this house were particularly eager to have a house that was exciting, both inside and out, and, at the same time, they wanted to hold construction costs to a minimum.

Knowing that out-of-the-ordinary building techniques invariably boost costs, the owners agreed on a plan to use only standard carpentry procedures, and no custom millwork. In addition they planned to do a good deal of the finishing work themselves. This included painting and staining the exterior and interior, and laying vinyl asbestos in the bedrooms and bathrooms.

Many of the ways in which costs were cut served to add rather than detract from the house—the exposed beam ceiling, the gypsum board walls accented with fir trim, the hardwood floors, the use of crystal instead of plate glass in the tall, narrow living room windows.

Because they specifically did not want a family room, the owners asked that the children's rooms be large and comfortable. Bathroom fixtures could be white rather than colored; the kitchen could be basic as long as it had a view.

The architects designed many finishing details to be done by the owners including the grillework on the front door and upstairs hall windows, the large bookcase in the living room, and the decks to the rear of the house.

Because the lot had been part of a garden belonging to the neighboring house, much of the landscaping was already in including several mature trees and shrubs.

DECK

MASTER
BEDROOM

LOFT

dn.

DRESSING &
BATH

OPEN TO
L.R. BELOW

BATH

HALL

BEDROOM

BEDROOM

UPPER FLOOR

DINING
ROOM

KITCHEN

STO. W.D.

Telephone

STUDIO

LIVING
ROOM

Clothes
Chute

up

ENTRY
HALL

dn.

Scale in feet
0   5   10

WALKWAY

CARPORT

LOWER FLOOR

OVERHEAD GALLERY *with a study area provides the high-ceilinged living room with contrast of a low ceiling over the fireplace.*

NO DOOR *between the dining room and kitchen, and no kitchen cabinet doors were specified; can be added later.*

THREE BEDROOMS *open off upstairs hallway. Door screen repeated on upstairs windows; rafters exposed.*

LOOKING DOWN from living room deck to garden. Patio bricks are 3½ inches wide, 11½ inches long, 1¾ inches thick, laid on sand. Raised bench outlines patio; beyond are the children's swing and sand box.

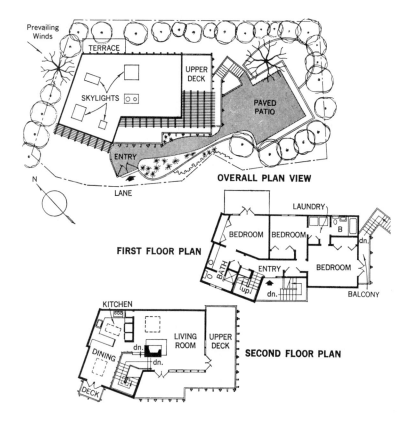

OVERALL PLAN VIEW

FIRST FLOOR PLAN

SECOND FLOOR PLAN

Three-level living

ARCHITECT: ROBERT W. HAYES

For three years this house stood on its hillside site in Sausalito, California, as a partly framed structure. It was planned as a much larger house, but construction was halted by legal action over housing density and access to the street when only one wing and part of a second had been framed.

The architect bought the skeleton, and without changing much of the basic structure, designed this three-bedroom, two-bath house for his family.

The major change from the original plan was to locate the living areas on the upper floor, where there is a good view of San Francisco Bay over rooftops and trees. Because the upper level is small, a small deck off the dining room and another around two sides of the living room were designed to make the rooms seem larger. The decks provide close-at-hand outdoor living space up where there's more sun.

ON UPPER DECK outside the living room, you can enjoy the view as well as the sun when patio below is tree-shaded. Deck is actually duckboards of redwood 1 by 4's on 2 by 3-inch stringers placed over roof.

on a heavily wooded site

HEARTH and fireplace decoration are precast, 250-pound panels of pebbles; dining area in background.

OPEN SCREEN of 2 by 2's on 4-inch centers and 2 by 4's on 2-foot centers separates dining area, stairwell.

TWO-STORY screened structure seems to enfold the fresh air, sky, and trees. Planned as part of the indoor-outdoor complex is the swimming pool just below. Paved area beside pool expands entertaining area.

A screened room two stories high

DESIGNER: JOHN I. MATTHIAS

ORIGINAL STRUCTURE was an old three-car garage. Basic garage frame remained the same during remodeling.

This uncommonly interesting house at one time was an uncommon three-car garage (see photo to left) on a wooded, hill section of an old estate in Pasadena, California.

But its interest lies less in its origins than in the environment it creates and the exciting quality it achieves by exploiting vertical space. Out from the shell of the original building came a two-story screen structure that enfolds airy space. It allows the main part of the house to be in touch with fresh air, sky, and trees that direct the eye upward. The outdoor room the design creates is another living room, dining room, party room, entry, and hallway. Planned as part of this indoor-outdoor complex is a swimming pool just below, which contributes to an atmosphere of carefree living.

Indoors, the house has a large, informal living-dining area and bedrooms that have the feeling of separate apartments, in contrast with the large group-living spaces. Foot traffic between parts of the house can move either indoors or outdoors.

Strategically located in the center of the house, the kitchen is handy for serving to the dining area or to the screened outdoor room (and to the pool beyond). While the living room and kitchen are usually left open to the screened outdoor room, sliding glass doors can close them in cold or rainy weather.

LUNCHING OUTDOORS, *your eye is led upward to tall trees and the sky. Plastic panels cut breeze slightly.*

LIVING ROOM *gives pleasant sense of horizontality in contrast to open vertical spaces to which it opens.*

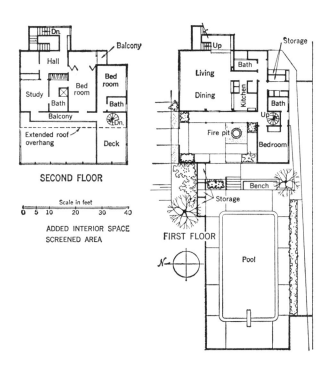

SECOND FLOOR

Scale in feet
0 5 10 20 30 40

ADDED INTERIOR SPACE
SCREENED AREA

FIRST FLOOR

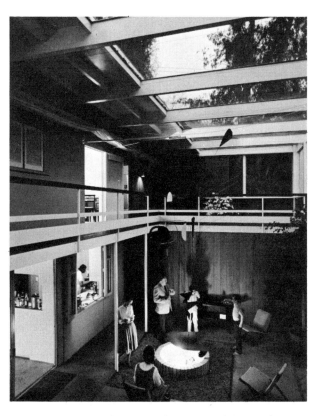

FLOOR PLANS *show the room layout of each floor and how the house relates to pool for indoor-outdoor living.*

FIREPIT GLOWS *during gathering outdoors. Above is second-story deck. Note the roof shelter for the balcony.*

DECK off family room and kitchen joins level lawn area which is also sunniest part of the garden.

Ingenuity preserved the lot's natural beauty

ARCHITECT: ANTON MUELLER

The design of this house is unusual mainly because it was the only way the architect could find to fit the house to the lot without altering the grade. (For exterior view, see page 27.)

The bedrooms are on the lower level, the living room is a level above, and the kitchen another level above that. The level part of the lot is at the front and is also the sunniest. This area is used as the main outdoor living area and is well screened from the street by trees. A covered entry bridge along one side of the house also provides some privacy from the neighbors on the north.

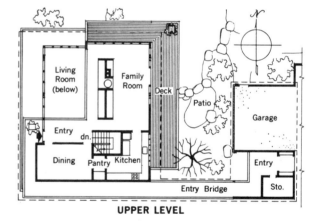

UPPER LEVEL

COVERED BRIDGE to house leads past level upper patio to front door on the opposite side of the house.

MIDDLE LEVEL

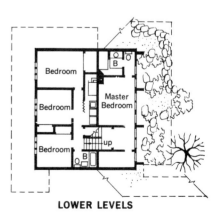

LOWER LEVELS

WOODSY SITE *was altered very little to make room for the house. Deck at the left is the front entry.*

Roomy, but kept within the budget

ARCHITECT: OTTO RITTER

Essentially a rectangle, this house is only 45 feet long and 28 feet wide. But within its two levels are three bedrooms, two baths, living room, dining room, kitchen, multi-purpose room, plus a two-story-high studio. The architect built it as his own home and by careful planning, managed to keep it within a moderate budget.

The living and dining areas open into the two-story studio space to make the house seem much larger than it is. The multi-use room is outside the children's bedrooms, tucked out of sight under the dining area (see plan), with access to a deck-covered play spot outside.

Here are some of the ways the architect pared down his cost: Selection of site meant little site preparation. A 4-foot modular design was used so standard panels of plywood and gypsum board could be used. Utility grade studs were used for all concealed framing. A roof overhang was eliminated. Crystal glass was used in all windows. Short lengths of lumber were used for flooring, and utility-grade knotty hemlock was used for the ceiling.

STAIRS *lead down from living room to lofty studio, which doubles as second living room for entertaining.*

HOUSE FITS *easily into its setting of native plants. Note that most windows face away from the street.*

Simple rectangle conceals three levels

ARCHITECTS: TROGDON-SMITH

This house in Spokane, Washington, occupies a moderately steep lot on which little of the grade or natural vegetation was disturbed. Designed as a simple rectangle, it doesn't reveal outwardly its three-level interior space which accommodates a family of three generations: grandmother, parents, and three children.

There are well separated areas for each age, and living room, dining room, kitchen, and studio on the middle level to be used by the entire family. Decks extend these rooms outside, and provide easy access to the garden. The entry level (not shown in the plans at right) contains a bedroom, bath, storage, utility room, garage.

ENTRY STEPS *and walk parallel drive to garage. Bank above walk planted with junipers; below with rock-plants.*

DECK *doubles size of the living room, especially during the summer; provides easy access to the garden.*

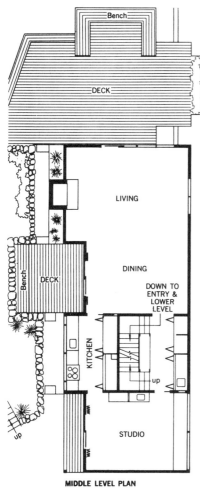

Bench

DECK

LIVING

DINING

DECK

Bench

DOWN TO
ENTRY &
LOWER
LEVEL

KITCHEN

up

up

STUDIO

MIDDLE LEVEL PLAN

Open Below

MASTER
BEDROOM

BATH

dn.

LAUNDRY

STORAGE

BATH

Skylight

Scale in feet

0   5   10

BEDROOM   BEDROOM

UPPER LEVEL PLAN

OPEN STAIRWAY, *with skylight above, is shown from the middle level.*

CEILING *in living room is 22 feet high, extends over part of deck. It and native pines cut sky glare. Master bedroom above shares this view.*

SIDING *of house goes right down to the footings. No exposed underpinnings on the down slope.*

This house is inside-out
ARCHITECTS: RICHARD PETERS AND PETER DODGE

Scale in feet
0   5   10   15   20

NORTH

Bath

Den

Bath

Up

Bedroom

Bedroom

LOWER LEVEL

Kitchen

Dining

Bath

Deck

Central Court

Entry

Dn.

Living

Deck

FIRST LEVEL

At first glance, the outside of this house is somewhat startling; windows and doors aren't quite where you expect them to be. But in this case you must go inside. Then everything explains itself. It's an inside-outside house.

Here are high windows and treetop views, a bay window that seats you in the trees, skylights overhead, open balconies to coax you out—and what the architects call a "light grabbing" central court, which functions like an interior room that's open to the sky. There are many ways this court can be used. It's an alternate route from living room to kitchen if the weather is good. It's an outdoor room private from the outdoor world. It's roomy; on good days it doubles the size of the living room.

The upper level is open and sunny, with natural daylight flowing in from overhead. Downstairs the plan is not open, but closed. The house was an award winner in an A.I.A.-Sunset Western Home Awards program.

ROOFLESS CENTER COURT *lets you look through, over to wooded slopes; dining room visible across the way.*

METAL FIREPLACE *has its own bay daylit by tall, narrow windows; living room is 15 by 15½ feet.*

Another inside-out idea

ARCHITECTS: IAN MACKINLAY & ASSOC.

As you move around in this house your eye moves to adjacent rooms and spaces, drawn there because the ceiling goes up or because space somehow turns a corner.

The owners are weather hounds, weather watchers—they love to catch the moods of storms and wind and be able to see the wind bending the trees. Their house was designed accordingly.

The house form is simple: essentially a vertical box with three living levels. The living room is only 16 by 22 feet, but rises the height of two stories with a great bay window that seems to extend the room out into the trees. A plastic skylight, set above the bay, brings in additional daylight from above. The living room ceiling of exposed joists is carried back over the adult's bedroom loft. A deck pushes out from the house to become an outdoor extension of indoor floors.

The house was an award winner in an A.I.A.-Sunset Western Home Awards program.

STAIRS *from parking deck lead down to generous entry deck at living level.*

DINING AREA *is under adults' sleeping loft; living room is two-story.*

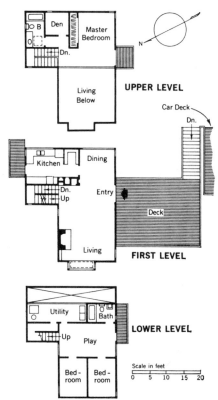

UPPER LEVEL

FIRST LEVEL

LOWER LEVEL

The wooded site was undisturbed

ARCHITECTS: CLEMENT CHEN & ASSOC.

The owners specifically desired a house with a large living room, open views of a wooded canyon, a separate dining room, glassed porch area that could be opened in the summer, a separate studio, the bedrooms upstairs. Above all, they did not want the trees disturbed.

To make the house look as if it had always been a part of the heavily wooded site, the plans called for re-sawn redwood to be used throughout, plus cedar shingle siding, plus large expanses of glass. A generous engawa extends the living area on this sloping site.

ENGAWA seems to extend living room floor outside, encompassing trees and planting areas next to windows.

WINDOW WALL of living room looks out on woodsy lot whose natural appearance was kept completely intact.

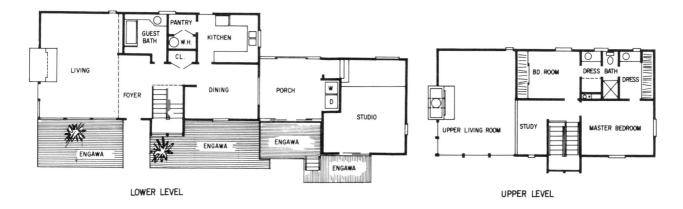

LOWER LEVEL

UPPER LEVEL

Three decks plus a mezzanine

ARCHITECTS: RICHARD DORMAN & ASSOC.

This house of 2,400 square feet gives a surprisingly spacious effect, due in part to the two-story high living room, an open staircase, and an all-purpose mezzanine that shares the view. The house achieves an interesting relationship of high and low areas by the use of exposed framing and medium-pitch roof. Projecting decks on two levels across the front of the house open the rooms to the outside. The house was an award winner in an A.I.A.-Sunset Western Home Awards program.

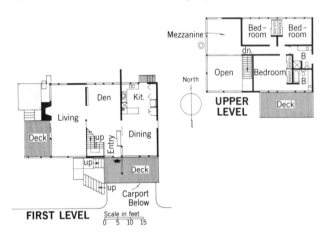

SLENDER TREES *soften look of glass walls in living room.*

Living with space and sunlight

ARCHITECT: LEROY B. MILLER

The interior of this house is a wonderful three-dimensional composition (or four-dimensional: up, down, sideways, plus daylight). The wall openings take your eye up or down and then into spaces. Clerestories on the street side bring in high daylight. The architect gave a townhouse facade to the street and placed decks and a terrace for outdoor living in the back. The house was an award winner in an A.I.A.-Sunset Western Home Awards program.

CLERESTORIES *on street side bring in high daylight.*

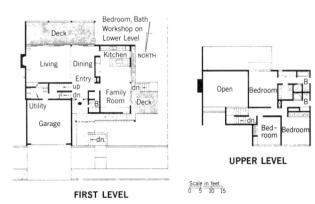

(See coverage of this house on page 50)

SMALL HOUSES FOR SMALL LOTS

To plan and build a house on a lot where every square foot counts tests the ingenuity not only of the architect, but that of the builder and the homeowner. How to establish privacy, how to enjoy outdoor living with the pleasure of a garden, how to live with spaciousness—all of these and other challenges require careful planning and imagination when you have a small lot to start with.

The magic and charm of a small house is not always evident from the outside. Blank facades and high walls or screens are often necessary in order to achieve a measure of privacy from close neighbors or a busy street; not until you get past the exterior "buffer zone" do the warmth and livability of the house become evident.

A small garden court may open the interior to the delights of the outdoors. Or, high windows may bring in overhead views of changing clouds, treetops tossing in the wind, distant skylines. Perhaps the interior is so arranged that one area seems to flow into another—from low ceilinged intimate rooms to lofty soaring galleries. Take note of the fresh and unusual approaches the houses in this chapter use to achieve spaciousness, light, and privacy.

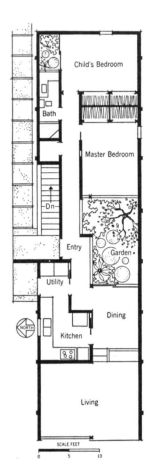

Child's Bedroom

Bath

Dn

Master Bedroom

Entry

Garden

Utility

Dining

NORTH

Kitchen

Living

SCALE FEET
0   5   10

THE FACADE *and downhill side of house are completely closed for privacy.*

Every foot counts

ARCHITECT: HOMER DELAWIE

This is a simple house on a 25-foot-wide hillside lot where all living and sleeping areas are confined to one floor. Storage and parking are provided below. Because of a nearby freeway and next-door apartments, the architect closed the south wall, except for translucent light panels. Light also enters from an interior garden court opening on the living area, master bedroom, and hallway. A window wall in the living room in the rear provides a harbor view. The house was an award winner in an A.I.A.-Sunset Western Home Awards program.

WINDOW WALL *in rear gives spacious effect to small living room; it also provides a view of the harbor.*

CENTRAL GARDEN, *seen from dining room, was planned like another room and brings in light and garden outlook.*

LOOKING FROM COURT *back into main house at dusk. Living-family room below, parents' bedroom above.*

The children live across the court

ARCHITECT: ROBIN BOYD

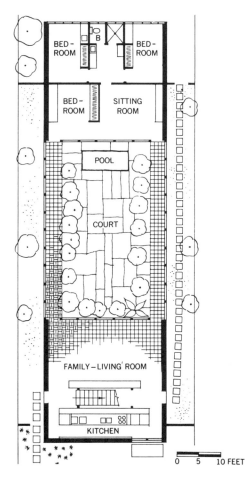

At the front and back of a 40-foot-wide lot, the architect placed two buildings, each about 28 feet square. The front has house entry and parents' bed-sitting room upstairs; cooking, dining, and family living at the garden level below. To the rear is a children's house with bedrooms, bath, and sitting room at garden level. But the magic of this house is what happens between buildings. Tall walls of glass connect the halves of the house and create a 40-foot garden court. The obscure glass establishes privacy. A mild climate permits the use of this interior court most of the year. A roofed walkway at each side of the court provides shelter from building to building.

LIVING-FAMILY ROOM *has open fireplace, brick end walls, and glass wall which looks out on the central court.*

TWO-STORY GLASS *of the living area gives effect that house is "floating" among the trees.*

Small...but open and lofty

ARCHITECTS: BUFF, STRAUB & HENSMAN

The owners wanted an effect of space and generous scale in their house, although it was to be small (1,400 square feet). Its hillside site, with its view toward mountains to the northeast, gave the architects an opportunity to let the house "float" among the trees.

Half the living area is a two-story room, with two-story glass, and half is one-story. Above, two bedrooms on a continuous balcony open onto the two-story space and the view. The bedrooms can be closed with translucent screens. With the exception of the den, all rooms can be opened to the flowing vertical space.

A deck opposite the entry to the living room is built around one of the existing oak trees adding to the effect of open and lofty spaces.

The house was an award winner in an A.I.A.-Sunset Western Home Awards program.

CEILING *over the living room creates sheltered area in contrast to open two-story space beyond.*

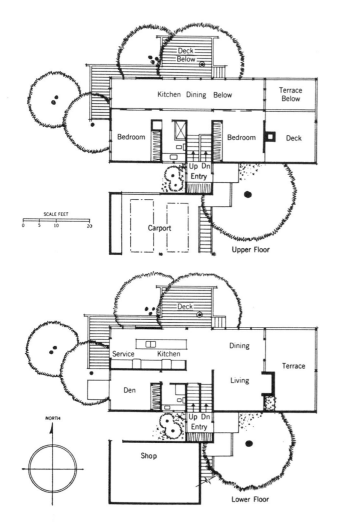

KITCHEN ISLAND *is long and includes eating counter at far end. Sliding screens to bedrooms are above.*

SLIDING PANELS, *on channels mounted 3 feet outside the glass, provide shade from afternoon sun.*

It's really a glass room in a garden

ARCHITECTS: KILLINGSWORTH, BRADY, SMITH AND ASSOC.

A glass pavilion set on a narrow ledge in the garden of an old estate in Laguna Beach, California, this small house (only 1,400 square feet) provides a secluded environment in intimate touch with the garden and with a clear view of the coastline below. (For another view of the exterior, see page 45.)

The floor plan is a simple rectangle, with studio-living-dining areas at one end, sleeping-bathing-cooking at the other. The house was pre-fabricated in nine bents—rigid in both directions, so glass could be used on all sides — and erected in 30 days. The house was an award winner in an A.I.A.-Sunset Western Home Awards program.

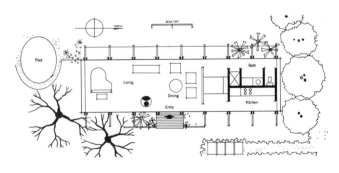

INTERIOR *is unbroken by walls except in the kitchen.*

CORNER *of living room blends right in with garden.*

ENTRY *is on landing between floors on uphill side.*

FOCAL POINT *of the living area is the brick hearth.*

VIEW TO DINING AREA. *Table straddles a floor-to-ceiling window, is suspended on side by wood hangers.*

Trim two-story

ARCHITECTS: ANDERSON & BELL

In just a little over 1,000 square feet of space, the architects fitted together a trim box of a house, with room for a beginning family and a minimum strain on the budget. It is stepped into a steep hill, 4 feet below grade on the uphill side, 4 feet above on the downhill side.

The house was kept simple enough so that the owner could do the carpentry himself. The steep grade of the slope allowed for building the carport at street level and for sheltering a terrace under it.

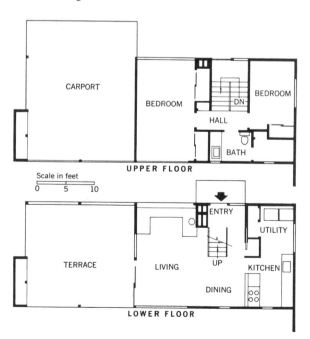

SEEN FROM LANAI, *the living room has 14-foot ceiling for spaciousness. Light from tall strip windows washes walls during day; roof-mounted floodlights illuminate the area at night.*

It has an almost sculptural quality

ARCHITECTS: MORSE AND TATOM

Although this is a small and low-cost house on a 45 by 100-foot lot, it achieves spaciousness, light, and privacy that are quite surprising. The plasticity of its form gives an almost sculptural quality.

The heart of the house is a lofty room, suffused with light and offering a variety of views of the nearby garden or the distant tree-tops and sky. Garden walls blank out any distracting nearby scenes and extend the interior space to the property line. A large old monkeypod tree (see cross-section sketch on opposite page) not only provides front garden and patio shade, but also privacy from the street.

This simple white house is distinctly regional. In its Honolulu location, it recognizes and accepts brilliant plant colors, bright sunlight, and changing shadows as design elements (characteristic also of much of the Western mainland), and makes architecture a background to them.

Materials are simple: concrete block walls washed with white cement, an olive-gray waxed concrete floor, an olive-yellow wood ceiling, bleached wood exterior trim and doors. Tall strip windows and skylights are balanced against glass walls and doors.

The living room has a 14-foot ceiling for spaciousness. A strip skylight washes the side wall with light during the day and is softly illuminated by roof-mounted floodlights at night. The skylight is set back under roof overhang for protection from the weather.

The house was an award winner in an A.I.A.-Sunset Western Home Awards program.

TWO OUTDOOR ROOMS —*patio and large lanai—add to livability and outdoor enjoyment of small house.*

KITCHEN *is partly obscured from view of dining room, foreground; patio through curtained doors at right.*

CROSS-SECTION SKETCH *shows how focal room reaches up for light; garden wall treated as part of house.*

SPACIOUS LIVING ROOM *opens directly onto garden deck in a pleasant indoor-outdoor relationship. A 12-foot window wall provides good interior lighting; entryway down steps at left is level with street.*

Gardener's house...craftsman's house

ARCHITECT: JOSEPH WESTON

Here is a house for a retired couple, for the amateur craftsman, for the hobby gardener, for the builder on a hillside, or for the small house planner building on a narrow beach or town lot.

The owners were all of these things. Furthermore, the man of the house, a retired architect, knew how to design a charming, warm, and livable house to serve these needs.

The site was a narrow 40 by 100-foot lot, fronted on the east by the street and sloping down from this level to the back property line (see plan on opposite page). It included three fine trees—a pine and oak in the front, a second oak to the rear. Raising the main living area provided a full story on the downhill side of the lot for a studio work area; opening it to the trees with windows front and rear gave it light and privacy.

The generous-sized entryway, on eye-level with the street, has stairs leading up to the living area, down to the studio.

With approximately 1,200 square feet of space, the living area includes a laundry room, a second bath, and on a slightly higher level over the carport, a guest bedroom for visiting children.

Plastic skylights insure good light even on dark days in the kitchen, baths, and laundry room.

The garden deck is fully protected from the street by trees, on the north by the entryway, and on the south by a lath and plastic screen. Hand hewn, random-spaced pergola beams overhead provide an effect of protection and a place for hanging plants.

Down the stairs from the entryway, the 800-square-foot studio is screened by a pierced, plywood panel. A door from the studio leads out to the back garden work area which is used entirely for plant cultivation.

All interior wall surfaces are ⅜-inch plywood painted white; the ceiling in the entry hall and upstairs living area is unpainted shiplap siding. In the downstairs studio, the walls are white, the floors unfinished plywood. The living area floors are carpeted except for baths, laundry, and kitchen.

GALLEY-TYPE KITCHEN *is convenient to dining area. Skylight adds a cheerful atmosphere. Balcony has plant shelves and a small, wall-hung, flip-up counter if the owners wish to eat outside.*

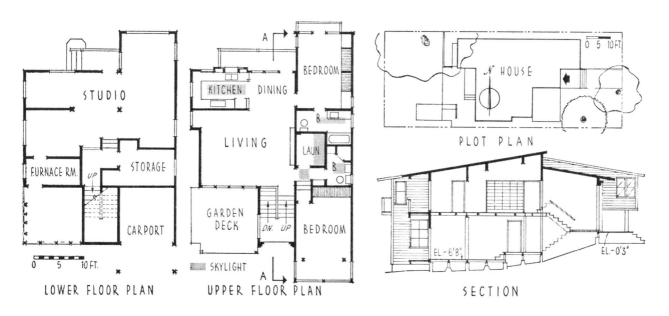

LOWER FLOOR PLAN

UPPER FLOOR PLAN

PLOT PLAN

SECTION

LIVING AREAS *are all upstairs, including a laundry with washer and dryer; lower floor has separate furnace and storage room. Difference in elevation between back of the house and street level is 9 feet.*

NARROW FRONT SECTION *of house makes neighbors seem farther away; steel frame is anchored to slope.*

A built-in garden works magic

ARCHITECT: ROSCOE WOOD

GARDEN COURT *is off living room; hallway to the left.*

A garden court and translucent walls contribute most to the spaciousness and livability of this small house on a narrow lot in Redondo Beach, California. Imagine it on any small subdivision lot, flat or sloping, and you have an answer to the problem of opening a house to the delights of the outdoors but still keeping it private from close neighbors.

The house has a steel pipe frame to float the front section over the sloping site. The rear section has concrete blocks helping to anchor the house to the slope. With only two windows on the south side, it is still pleasantly light inside because of the translucent wall (burlap embedded in glass-fiber-reinforced plastic, with an outer layer of glass to prevent weather deterioration). Louvered windows catch the prevailing sea breeze helping to control the heat on hot summer days. The windows form the upper section of window wall facing the sea.

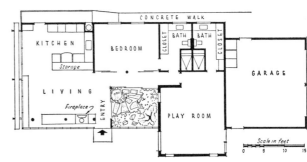

CONCRETE WALK *from garage leads to the kitchen door.*

Compact and inexpensive

ARCHITECT: MARY LUND DAVIS

This 800-square-foot house has exteriors which are straightforward and interiors which are simple and uncluttered. Both of these elements are characteristic of a thoughtful design for prefabrication. The house is intended for a small family or for a retired couple. The exterior features prefab panel sections that reveal post-and-beam framing. The house was an award winner in an A.I.A.-Sunset Western Home Awards program.

EXTERIOR *features panel sections that reveal post-and-beam framing.*

Living-dining is up top

ARCHITECTS: DONALD J. BATCHELDER AND JOSEPH F. DROSIHN

Situated on a steep site, this small house (1,400 square feet) works well because it uses space vertically—living, cooking, dining areas on the top level, sleeping on the two levels below. Entry is by steps and a deck to the middle level, by bridge to the top level. The house was an award winner in an A.I.A.-Sunset Western Home Awards program.

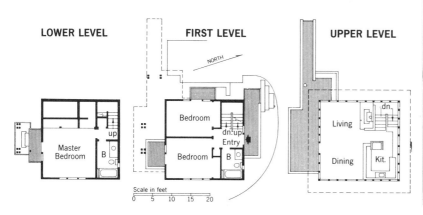

PLAN AREA *kept small not to cover site; entry is at middle level.*

LIVING AREAS *are elevated into trees.*

It uses pole framing

ARCHITECTS: DAVID R. GARCIA & JOHN W. COLE

Designed to fit on a wooded sloping site with a minimum of tree removal and grading, this square house uses pole framing to lift it up among the trees. The treated wood poles seem to become part of the forest setting.

Car storage and the main entry are on the lower level, entry to the main level is through a central core stairwell skylit from above. The house was an award winner in an A.I.A.-Sunset Western Home Awards program.

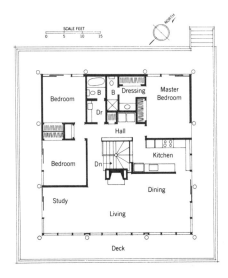

WOOD POLES *accommodate house to the site by elevating it above slope.*

Tailored to its climate

ARCHITECTS: JOHN ANDERSON AND ASSOC.

To fit its Northwest climate, this house features a large deck with overhead roof frame. The deck's roof frame was designed with the idea that it could be covered with translucent plastic or with vines to make a secluded out-door living area. The house has a central hall floor plan and a large unfinished lower floor opening onto a roofed lower outdoor area. The house was an award winner in an A.I.A.-Sunset Western Home Awards program.

ENTRY *is on portion of large sun deck beyond carport.*

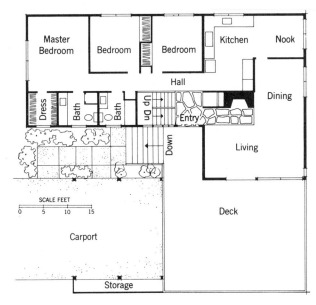

(*See coverage of this house on page 64*)

HOUSES FOR COUNTRY, MOUNTAINS, AND SEASHORE

The desire to get away from it all, to enjoy all year long the rugged beauty of a site, or simply to retire to a secluded spot—whatever your motive —a house in the country, mountains, or at the seashore can reflect its setting in a design that is casual and free-flowing. It can ramble over its site or it can be compact for minimum house-keeping. Interiors can complement this atmosphere of relaxed and easy living. In short, this kind of house can be a bit more unusual in design than its suburban counterpart.

Unlike the typical weekend cabin, a house in an out-of-the-way setting must offer comforts for full-time living. Minor inconveniences that might be bearable during a brief holiday (makeshift sleeping arrangements, chilly or damp rooms, snow or water glare) will soon become major irritations if you try to live with them the year around.

As with any house in a rural setting, provisions for storage should be ample for all sorts of possibilities—a sudden power failure, an unusual cold spell, even a snow-storm that isolates you for a few days.

The houses shown in this chapter are especially noteworthy because they were built to be compatible with the environment *without* any need for undue alteration of the site.

CHARM of adobe ranch house is summed up in this view from parking court. Despite the nearly blank facade—for privacy and protection from the afternoon sun—house seems warm and inviting.

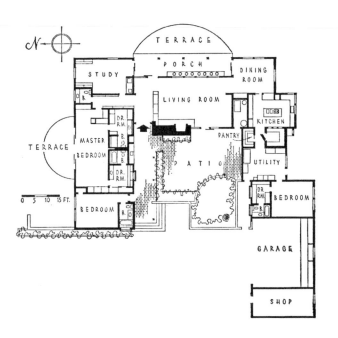

In the true Western

DESIGNER: CLIFF MAY

With careful attention to the site and climate and to the owners' needs, this large house in the country exploits the traits of the traditional Western ranch house. It is a house with a timeless quality. It embodies the easy informality, the sense of shelter, easy movement indoors and out, and warm materials traditional with the ranch type house.

The site is a knoll. Access is from the road to the West, the only side where the site does not give complete privacy. On this side, privacy is achieved by an almost blank, but not unfriendly facade, fronted by the parking area. This west-facing facade also minimizes the effect of the hot afternoon sun. Other windows that face west are sheltered by wide overhangs.

The owners made sure their main outdoor living area —off the living and dining rooms, and used for enter-

NIGHT VIEW *taken from terrace shows relation of dining room to living room (right), kitchen (background).*

LIVING ROOM OPENS *to patio (at left) and intimate garden; entry is behind the storage divider.*

STUDY *combines quality of library and sitting room; dropped ceiling creates quiet area at library end.*

ranch house tradition

taining—faced east to provide afternoon shade. They also wanted a good view of the wooded slopes from the kitchen southward and a terrace off the master bedroom on the north. The site was to be disturbed by grading as little as possible, and particularly the fine old oak trees were to be preserved.

Every room in this house except the kitchen opens to an outdoor living area. Movement in and out is easy, through large passageways onto floor and terrace surfaces at the same level.

The living room separates the bedroom wing from the cooking and eating wing. It opens to two paved outdoor living areas, the more intimate patio and the more expansive east-facing terrace, for a choice of sun or shade any time of the day. You can enter either wing without passing through the center of the house.

COOK ISLAND *in kitchen puts plenty of counter space within easy reach; sliding doors close off this area.*

FIRST FLOOR

SECOND FLOOR

FIREPLACE WELL provides small conversation area in large living room. Dining area is above with pass-through to the kitchen.

SLIDING doors between bedrooms can be removed when children leave home.

Designed to handle six youngsters

ARCHITECTS: JAMES M. WIDRIG AND DAVID H. WRIGHT

A two-story country house is designed to meet the needs of six children and at the same time to make a busy mother's job as easy and pleasant as possible. Living room, dining room, kitchen, and activity rooms are large to fulfill a big family's need for elbow room, but they contain a minimum of dust-catching, wasted space.

The 17-acre site of this house is out in the country, and the children find much to do outdoors. This makes playtime a delight for the children, but provides a bundle of laundry for their mother. Anticipating this problem, the architects put a laundry-sewing room on the second floor, near the bedrooms.

When the older children leave for college, the family will need fewer bedrooms. At that time, the partitions that now divide three large bedrooms into six small ones will be removed.

WOODSY SETTING for a house designed to keep housework at minimum.

SUNNY DECK runs the length of the house; is accessible from rooms on both living, sleeping ends.

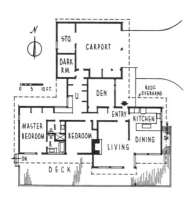

Simplicity and privacy

ARCHITECT: JOHN STORRS

In the wooded hills of Portland, this house seems as appropriate to its site as the trees themselves. This comes partly from its simple design and quiet, natural materials, and partly from its emphasis on privacy. At the front of the house, only the kitchen and den face the street. The south wall is almost entirely of glass. It opens onto a generous deck that serves as a light and sunny outdoor living area amid surrounding forest.

COVERED ENTRY, kitchen, and carport face the street.

DECK adds to space of living area; dining room to left.

HOUSE SITS at base of wooded slope, which shades it from afternoon sun; fenced pasture in foreground.

Retirement house in a rural setting

ARCHITECT: MARIO CORBETT

Compact and with its areas carefully related, this small country house is a good example of design specifically intended for the needs of a retired couple. (For exterior view see page 59.) The combination entry hall-dining area makes it possible to have a choice of formal or informal living with a minimum of housekeeping and wasted space. The house reflects its rural setting in simplicity of line and materials. It is open to a view, yet it achieves the effect of enclosure desirable in an isolated home. It is oriented to balance sun and shade.

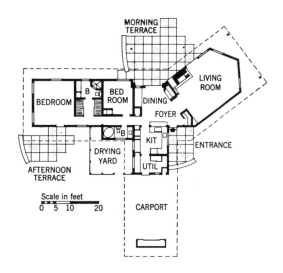

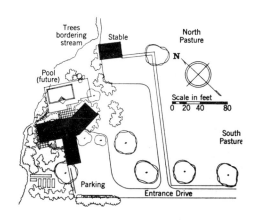

FOYER-DINING ROOM, *seen from living room, is informal gathering place; kitchen is beyond the counter.*

END WALL *of living room creates shelter and shade while providing view; note the lofty ceiling.*

PAVED AREA *is ample for lounging, walking. From bench in foreground you watch activity on putting green (at right). Covered section of patio is just outside kitchen, and next to family room.*

Relaxed living for the entire family

ARCHITECTS: TUCKER AND SHIELDS

A changing pattern of living for the owners is reflected in this country house. When their children were smaller, the owners lived in a two-story town house in Seattle, Washington. In their new home, rooms are all on one level and open on enclosed garden space. This makes for relaxed living, easy entertaining, and, most important, minimum maintenance.

Big front doors emphasize a welcome feeling at the end of a covered entry walk. Inside the entry hall, they look out at a garden court consisting of a lily pool and vine maples. The family room also looks out on an enclosed garden and has space for dancing and for enjoying family hobbies. From a roofed deck adjoining the living area, there is a view of the Cascades.

FROM THE STREET, *the house is barely seen; it will be even more secluded as plants grow up. Concrete walk around off-street guest parking leads to an entry gate which is framed by birch trees.*

FAMILY ROOM *has ample space for dancing and for enjoying family hobbies. Sliding glass doors lead to roofed deck which provides additional living space and also spectacular view of the Cascades.*

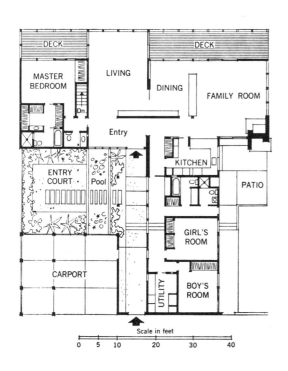

PARENTS' BEDROOM WING *is off by itself but still close to living area. Children's rooms can be shut off.*

SLIDING WINDOW *and counter-height shelf beyond were designed as pass-through from kitchen to patio area.*

ENTRY-ROAD SIDE *of house is private; house turns open side toward the mountain. View shows setting of house; nearby hills do not block view. Roof-level changes indicate the different house areas.*

Each indoor area has a

ARCHITECT: ROGER LEE

OUTDOOR AREAS match each room; living and sleeping areas are separate, linked together by entry hallway.

In Yreka, California, you naturally turn a house, if possible, to view Mount Shasta to the southeast. You also plan it for a climate of strong prevailing westerly winds, damp winters with perhaps two feet of snow, and 80° to 95° on summer days.

This medium-sized house does all of these things. The owners wanted a free-flowing house where they could entertain comfortably indoors and out. Their site has a view on all sides, which the house design takes full advantage of. With outdoor living and garden areas as varied as you can imagine, the demarcation between indoors and outdoors is often hardly noticeable. These areas, each matched to specific indoor spaces, range in scale from the intimate to the landscape of cosmic proportion. There is a small, sky-lit entry garden with a wall as backdrop; an enclosed garden court (off the guest bedroom); a garden patio off the master bedroom, elements of which the kitchen and study also share; a covered terrace off the dining room, easily accessible from the living room; and a terrace foreground to a wide living room vista of valley and mountains culminating in towering, snow-capped Mount Shasta.

The owners do not have children living at home, but the house provides for guest sleeping. The living and sleeping areas are treated as separate houses. This is clearly expressed in the roof configuration. An entry hallway links the two areas together and also minimizes foot traffic through rooms.

TERRACE *off master bedroom (right), faces morning sun. Glass doors (straight ahead) lead to the study.*

COMPACT KITCHEN *is easy to work in, can open or close to entry, patio, dining room (background).*

matching outdoor living area

FOLDING DOORS *close off study from living room. High ceiling, cove lighting gives study an open feeling.*

DRAMATIC SWEEP *of high living room and glass wall open to view. Lower dining room ceiling balances effect.*

PEAKED UNITS of house have plenty of daylight even when the snow is deep; the view is never obscured.

You can ski right over the carport

DESIGNER: DAVID TUCKER

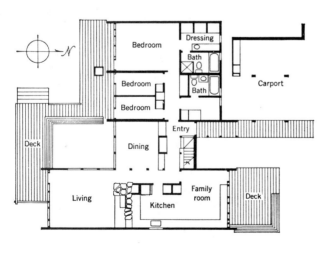

PLAN VIEW

At first glance this mountain house may appear to be three A-frames pushed together, almost like separate cabins with one larger cabin slightly off to one side. They're all joined together, however, and form this home in Alpine Meadows, California. The largest of the peaked units includes the living room, family room, and kitchen; the smaller units contain the bedrooms.

The lofty quality of the peaked areas was balanced with changes of level and space. Lofts were put over the kitchen and in the children's room, and the dining room was dropped one step to give it a ceiling of conventional height.

Many features were included to make mountain living more comfortable. Electric heating wires under the slate, for example, melt the snow on the entry walk. There's a bench just inside the front door where you can sit to take off or put on ski boots or overshoes. An adjoining closet has a warm air vent to dry snowy or rain-damp clothing. A window up near the ceiling peak in the play loft can be opened to release excessive heat in summer; in winter a return air duct draws heated air back for recirculation.

VIEW OF MOUNTAINS *is unobstructed by cross beams.*

LIVING ROOM *has blend of redwood, cedar, Douglas fir.*

COUNTER *extends from family room to the kitchen.*

SUMMER VIEW *shows front of house with carport, entry.*

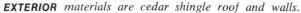

EXTERIOR materials are cedar shingle roof and walls.   *COUNTER with cook top separates living room, kitchen.*

All-year mountain living

ARCHITECT: JAMES D. MORTON

Taking full advantage of the view was more important than being close to the road, so the owners built their house toward the back of the lot on the uphill side. To gain even more height for the view from the living areas, these were put on the upper floor, the bedrooms below (see plan). Because all the materials had to be carried up the hill, the house was designed to be built from small wood members, and no large beams were used. The telephone pole stock used to support the deck was carried up the hill by a bulldozer. The poles were laid across the bulldozer scoop and tied on at both ends. Concrete was also carried up in the scoop.

A generous 3½-foot overhang on the roof gives protection from sun glare during the snow season. The deck shown in the exterior photographs is used in summer for outdoor living; in winter it protects the main entry below. No water from rain or melting snow drips down through the 2 by 6-inch decking as it's caught underneath in plywood panels sprung in between the deck members and carried off to a concealed gutter.

ENTRY at right; track device for heavy loads, at left.

UPPER LEVEL

Deck — Living-dining — Kitchen — Bath — Bedroom

LOWER LEVEL

Bedroom — Storage — Entry — Spiral — Bedroom — Covered entry deck

LIVING-DINING ROOM has glass wall on both sides. The kitchen is beyond the low door at left.

Framed with steel

ARCHITECT: DAVID THORNE

The owners of this mountain house were very conscious of the rugged beauty of their secluded site and did not want it disturbed. The architect worked out a structural design in steel that would support the entire house on seven concrete pylons rising from the rock underneath. Only one small cedar had to be removed. Otherwise, existing trees were permitted to penetrate deck areas and overhangs; a huge sugar pine shades kitchen and living area windows on the west. The house has a double set of overhangs for added protection from the sun.

STEEL STRUCTURE ties house and deck to rocky slope.

DECK with laminated surface stretches into space.

ROOFED DECK *runs length of south side of house facing the water; living-sleeping areas overlook it.*

Gracious living at the water's edge

ARCHITECTS: KIRK, WALLACE, McKINLEY, AND ASSOC.

Located on Puget Sound in Washington, this house is full of ideas for bringing the interior into contact with the waterside site.

A roofed deck runs the length of the house that faces the ocean. The den, living-dining room, and master bedroom overlook it. The deck is both usable for an outdoor living area and as an exterior passageway. The deep overhang of the roof not only cuts down on afternoon glare but provides a substantial shelter so the owners can be outside even on stormy days.

The interior spaces are arranged sensibly and with great freedom despite the rigid modular structural system. A central roof monitor reaches up to bring overhead light into the living area. The fireplace alcove offers a conversational retreat that contrasts with the openness of the living room.

An entry bridge through a garden on the landward side of the house is roofed for protection against the weather. The floor plan also places utility, storage, and service areas on this side. The house was an award winner in an A.I.A.-Sunset Western Home Awards program.

RAISED CEILING SECTION *of living room allows for clerestory daylighting on all four sides.*

ENTRY BRIDGE *becomes a deck, roofed against the weather; entrance is at the center (background).*

__THE DUNES__ to seaward side of the house bloom with wildflowers and silver-green grasses in the spring.

This house braves the sea wind

ARCHITECT: EDWARD J. LA BELLE

__NORTH SIDE__ of house receives brunt of cold north wind, has only one narrow window in bathroom.

A year-around house in a summer-cottage setting was what the owners specified to their architect. In designing for such a setting, the architect's major problem was wind, which assumes gale proportions along this exposed coastal site in fall and winter. To combat the wind, the seaward roof line was kept low. The large expanse of glass in the center of the weather side of the house is set back well under the roof overhang for protection. On the sides, wing walls extend out to act as wind baffles. All windows except the louvered bathroom windows have fixed panes with ventilating panels. The house assumes the sheltering air of a chalet, characteristic where the elements are severe.

The degree of comfort demanded of a permanent house is necessarily greater than that tolerated in a summer-only cottage. The heating system in this house is one example. The major heat source is an oil-fired low pressure hot water system with the boiler housed in the garage. The living rooms use baseboard hot water heat, but bath and dressing rooms have radiant heat in the floor. The double fireplace has an extra large 21 by 21-inch flue and a 22-foot draw.

The rain gutters extend out beyond the sides of the roof, both as a decorative element and to increase their capacity, to lessen water splash and stain on exterior walls. Downspouts lead into a drainfield which runs into the dunes, emptying into large drums which are buried in the sand.

EFFICIENT KITCHEN *is as compact as ship's galley.*

FIREPLACE *divides the living room into two areas.*

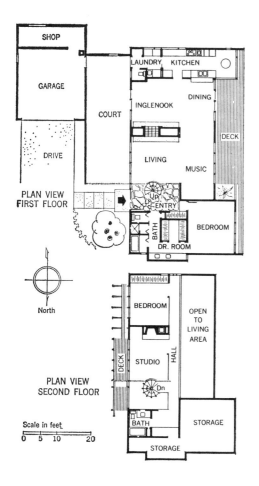

PLAN VIEW
FIRST FLOOR

SHOP

GARAGE

LAUNDRY   KITCHEN

INGLENOOK   DINING

COURT

DRIVE

LIVING   MUSIC

DECK

UP
ENTRY

BATH

DR. ROOM

BEDROOM

North

PLAN VIEW
SECOND FLOOR

BEDROOM

OPEN
TO
LIVING
AREA

DECK

STUDIO   HALL

Dn

BATH

STORAGE

STORAGE

Scale in feet
0   5   10   20

LOOKING TOWARD KITCHEN *and pass-through; there is
direct access to garage from living area to the left.*

CRESCENT-SHAPED DUNE *holds house; ice plant keeps sand from shifting. Curved walk leads to beach.*

It sits on a sand dune

ARCHITECT: LUTAH MARIA RIGGS

This house sits on a sand dune, almost completely surrounded by decks which widen out for outdoor living space to the front and the rear.

Each bedroom has a bath and each bath has an outside entrance so sand isn't trailed through the house.

Most of it can be washed off outside under a hot shower so it doesn't drain into the septic tank. The fireplace is on the street side so the living room has an uninterrupted view of the ocean. Sitting in the living room, all you can see beyond the deck is water.

GLASSED-IN END *of deck makes protected outdoor area.*

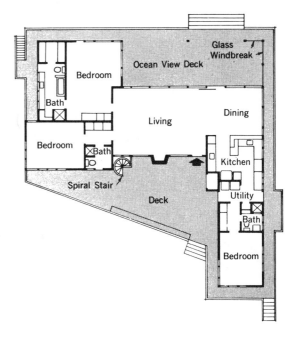

DINING AREA *looks out on beach. Windows are draped with matchstick bamboo over rayon.*

ON GLOOMY DAYS, *owners can turn their backs on ocean to enjoy scene of mountains beyond fireplace.*

Four levels on a lakeside

ARCHITECTS: BLAIR AND ZAIK

Although this two-story house fronts the water on its actual location, its basic design is good for any location where the view is directed downward. Four levels inside the house adapt to the sloping site and allow for separation of activities of adults and children. Living and dining areas face the view. A wide overhang on the roof eliminates much of the sky glare. A glass wall facing the water helps to balance the light. The house was an award winner in an A.I.A.-Sunset Western Home Awards program.

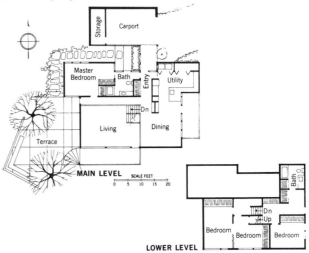

OUTDOOR DECKS *are visible in this view of the house.*

Living house and sleeping house

ARCHITECTS: HOOPER, OLMSTED & EMMONS

Floating comfortably over its site, this country house uses a living house-sleeping house pavilion-type plan, but one bedroom is in the living element. Rooms open to floor-level, roofed decks, which join the two sections.

The house is carefully oriented for maximum sunshine on the living side of the house. Grading was kept to a minimum. The house was an award winner in an A.I.A.-Sunset Western Home Awards program.

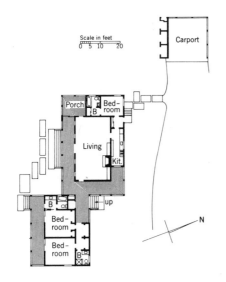

HIGH, GLAZED GABLE *provides the living unit with natural light.*

(See coverage of this house on next page)

HOUSES FOR DESERT REGIONS

The houses in this chapter reflect the careful planning and thoughtful consideration required for living in a desert climate. Construction techniques differ in many ways from the ones most frequently employed in other regions. The building materials alone—adobe, brick, concrete—require heavier foundations than are needed with frame construction, and often more specialized masonry skills. In addition, the electrical wiring and plumbing installation with these types of materials are usually more costly.

A house for year-round desert living must be designed to protect against possible low temperatures as well as to combat extreme heat. Although masonry construction is the traditional approach to one measure of climate control, it alone is not always the answer. Keeping a house cool and/or controlling the sun call for numerous special defenses: heavy shake roofs, tiled roofs, wide roof overhangs, overhead trellises, shutters for windows, double walls, and, in many cases, air conditioning.

TRELLIS over major outdoor living area is roof line extension that helps reduce sky glare in living room.

Built-in defenses against the desert sun

ARCHITECTS: CALVIN C. STRAUB AND DENIS P. KUTCH

As you can see from the exterior view on the previous page, this house comes very close to being a part of its site. Stone used for main bearing elements and for retaining walls was found on the site, and its use does much to accomplish what the owners wanted: a house that all but disappears into the hillside.

It's also a house designed for its desert climate. There are numerous defenses against the sun: stone piers that help block the early morning and late afternoon sun, wide roof overhangs, overhead trellises. But it's not an inward-turning house that shuts out the desert. Rather it welcomes the view through extensive window walls and sliding glass doors that open onto rock-paved or concrete patios. The end wall of the entry hall is glass, so as you approach the front door you can look out over the valley and to mountains in the distance.

Landscaping has been kept to a minimum. It consists mostly of encouraging the native vegetation that grows on the site. The house was an award winner in an A.I.A.-Sunset Western Home Awards program.

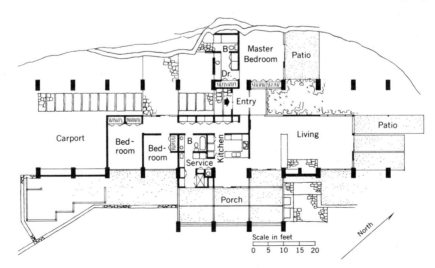

STONE PIERS are supporting elements of the house, indicated in the plan by solid black rectangles.

DIVIDER *back of sofa separates the living-dining areas.*   **KITCHEN** *opens onto covered porch; dining area at right.*

STONE RETAINING WALL *curves around hill, passes through master bedroom; roof overhang shades room.*

HOUSE, GARDEN WALLS *are burnt adobe with a light, surface wash to blend with the desert, mountains.*

Tile and burnt adobe

ARCHITECT: BENNIE M. GONZALES

Built with tile and burnt adobe, this house is a good example of the influence of territorial architecture on contemporary design.

The house and garden walls are burnt adobe with a light, off-white surface wash that helps to blend with desert and mountains. Floors throughout the house are 1⅜ by 8 by 12-inch clay tile. Tiled awning-like devices over the windows help to cut out the sun and glare. Landscaping was kept to mainly native plants and rocks.

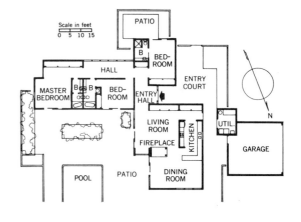

FIREPLACE *is divider between living, dining areas.*

TILED AWNINGLIKE DEVICES *over windows cut out sun.*

VIEWED FROM STREET: *Carport with half of gate open, breezeway, and main living area of house.*

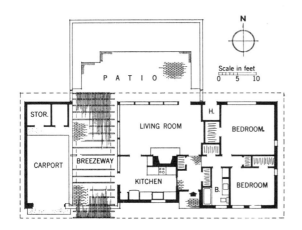

A breezeway patio

ARCHITECT: GORDON MAAS LUEPKE

The design of this small house in Tucson sensibly and pleasantly assembles architectural elements that keep it cool in a hot summer climate. Basically, it makes use of a device that is often too windy and chilly for many afternoons or evenings in many other areas: the breezeway patio. The spaced-lath overhead gives the brick-paved patio filtered shade but lets the breezes through. The patio is completely shaded by the house until mid-morning, and from midafternoon to evening by the carport roof.

LOOKING TOWARD *front wall, carport, from patio.*

LATH OVERHEAD *gives filtered shade to the patio.*

HIGH-CEILINGED *living room with dining balcony can be opened to desert; shutters control sun, glare.*

Its walls are masonry and glass

ARCHITECT: BENNIE M. GONZALES

When asked about the design of this house, the owner-architect replied that he and his wife wanted an informal house with a strong regional quality, built of materials reminiscent of what was used in Arizona in earlier days.

Viewed from a distance, the house appears at first to be a cluster of houses within a walled compound, somewhat suggesting an old hacienda. Still, as these photographs show, there was no attempt to re-create any past Southwest architectural style. Concrete slump block is used for both house and garden walls. Floors inside and exterior walks and patios are of burnt adobe blocks. Interior floors have a rich, almost leatherlike patina achieved by treating the adobe bricks with an oil stain, then sealing and waxing.

FIREPLACE opening high for view from dining balcony.

GALLERY runs width of house, is used for art display.

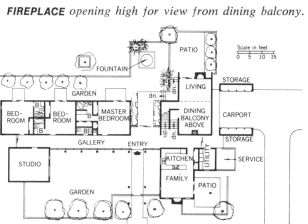

FOUR SEPARATE use areas are joined by long gallery.

FOUNTAIN seen from entry; heard in bedrooms, patio.

ROOF SLOPES and variations in ceiling heights help to create the illusion of a cluster of houses.

OUTSIDE GARDEN WALL *of burnt adobe is desert; inside, an easily-maintained oasis with brick paving.*

Oriented to thwart the sun

DESIGNER: J. R. SCHIBBLEY

This house makes good sense in its extremely warm climate. Notice how the house is oriented in the plan below. The patio, the pool, both bedrooms, and all sizable stretches of glass wall face northeast. They catch some sun early in the day, but the house stands between them and the hot sun that beats down in late afternoon.

Thick walls of burnt adobe provide excellent insulation. The white roof reflects sun heat. The house is only about 1,575 square feet, but there is no waste space. A burnt adobe wall extends from the house to enclose the outdoor living area. It also sets definite limits on the amount of garden to be maintained.

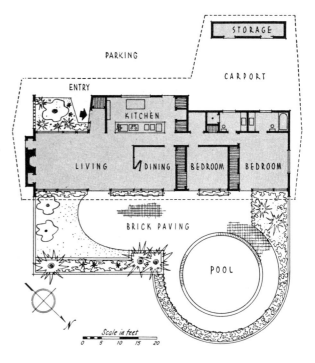

LIVING, DINING *areas open onto terrace, swimming pool.*

HOUSE seems a part of the desert with its thick adobe walls and heavy shake roofs over each pavilion.

It blends with its desert surroundings

ARCHITECT: BENNIE M. GONZALES

Admirably suited to the desert, this burnt adobe utilizes a two-pavilion concept to separate the main living and entertaining areas from the sleeping room; joining the two is a long, glass-walled hall (see plan).

The thick adobe walls, heavy shake roofs over each pavilion, and ceiling insulation inside all serve to protect the house against desert heat and cold.

The floors throughout the house are of particular interest. They're common brick laid closed-joint on a dry mortar bed over a termite-treated subgrade. The mortar bed was sprinkled with water, the brick was laid, then fine sand and cement were brushed into the joints and the surface was sprinkled. The finished floors were cleaned, sealed, and waxed.

LIVING-DINING-KITCHEN *area is essentially one room.*

ARCHED *window, fireplace in corner of living room.*

ARCH leads from pool garden to a shaded lower lanai on north side; above, deck surveys desert, mountains.

Multi-level living in the desert

ARCHITECTS: AMBROSE, SWANSON & ASSOC.

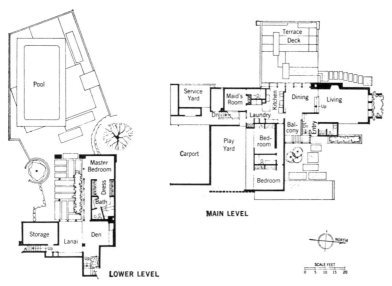

Pool

Master
Bedroom

Dress

Bath

Storage   Lanai   Den

Up

LOWER LEVEL

Terrace
Deck

Service
Yard

Maid's
Room

Kitchen

Dining   Living

Up

Dn

Laundry

Bal-
cony

Entry

Carport

Play
Yard

Bed-
room

Bedroom

MAIN LEVEL

NORTH

SCALE FEET
0   5   10   15   20

An undulating site, the severe summer climate, and the owners' desire to combine Southwestern tradition with their own distinctive needs—these were the conditions that made this house.

A four-level plan solved the site problem. Masonry construction is not only traditional, it is sensible as a sun control. There was one sun control conflict: The best view also looked into the setting sun. This was resolved in favor of the view; shutters close off the glass for the brief period when the sun is low in the west.

The cross-shaped plan evolved from separating the house into areas for parents, children, living-dining activities, services. The house was an award winner in an A.I.A.-Sunset Western Home Awards program.

VERTICAL PANELS *shut out most of early morning and late afternoon summer sun from the glass wall.*

LARGE FIREPLACE *dominates west wall of living room. Dining room (background) above living room floor level.*

KITCHEN *opens to deck on west (at second floor level on this side of house), has same view as dining room out over desert. Note roof overhang and shutters on the glass wall for protection from sun.*

FOUNTAIN is focal point of a large paved area for outdoor living. Entry through arched door at left.

In the Arizona territorial tradition

DESIGNER: DICK McNEILL

Built in and of the desert, this adobe house has the natural desert as landscaping outside, but within its walls it discloses a delightful verdant contrast.

The center of the house is a classical enclosed patio, in the style that has come to be known as Arizona territorial. Paved with brick, furnished with a tiled fountain, and planted with colorful bloom, it is the focus of the house. The rooms grouped around it on three sides share its garden effect, and seem the larger for opening onto it with wide sliding glass doors.

On the south side, two of the bedrooms share another walled garden, planted with lawn. This provides a private sunning area and enlarges these rooms with a garden outlook.

Burnt adobe, left natural, is as satisfactory a complement for the patio garden as for the natural desert landscape you see when you approach the house. Inside, natural or painted, adobe is a friendly setting for materials, accessories the owners had collected from Mexico.

MASTER BATH *door opens to small, landscaped patio.*   **FIREPLACE-BARBECUE** *is between living, dining areas.*

PATIO *extends space of living room, its natural adobe walls repeating the inside wall surface.*

A double wall cools this house

ARCHITECT: ROBERT J. PETERSON

To cope with its desert climate, this house employs a climate-control device worth study: the double wall. It consists of a wood-slat grille that covers most of the south facade, several feet out from the main house wall. The grille keeps sun and most of the glare away, but does not entirely block the view. Overhead the roof extends nearly to this line, but leaves an opening for air circulation. Behind, the main wall is masonry, or—farther back—glass that looks out on shade gardens. East and west walls are blank masonry to keep out heat.

WALL *of wood-slat grille fronts main wall of masonry.*

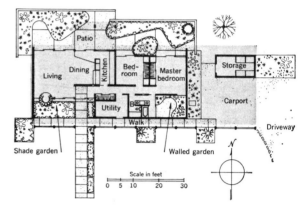

Summer freshness...winter warmth

ARCHITECT: GEORGE W. CHRISTENSEN

The principal materials in this house contribute to its coolness without seeming cold to the eye. The adobe that forms the walls is an excellent insulator against desert heat, yet it looks warm and friendly. The tile floor has a mellow earth color and is cool underfoot. There's more to the charm of this house than its materials. One part of its appeal lies in a comfortable and informal layout, with living at the center and sleeping in two wings to form a U-shape around a patio with a swimming pool. Outside, adobe brick courses add to the charm.

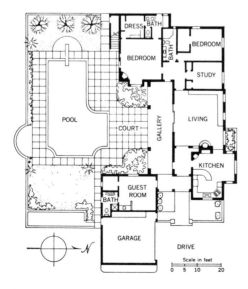

TILED ROOF *provides shade for south-facing windows.*

COMFORT AND LIVABILITY
IN YOUR HOME

Upon entering some houses, you are immediately aware of a certain charm, a visual warmth that seems to radiate from the surroundings. Frequently this is because of the pleasing airiness of the rooms or because natural light seems to give the living areas a special glow. The house in the photograph above features a high-ceiling, daylit entry. Contrasting with this open feeling is the intimacy of the book-lined main hallway (right) and the small seating alcove (foreground).

Many such ideas can be a planned part of the house, but even after you've lived in the house awhile and become aware of certain desires and needs, further custom touches can be added (room dividers, sliding glass doors to make a room seem larger, artificial lighting, bringing the garden indoors, use of skylights, sun controls, use of screens for privacy). This chapter contains a wide variety of ideas for making your house more comfortable, livable, and inviting.

Skylights, clerestory windows, window walls

Daylight is an old friend we know only too well. We generally accept it as casually as the air we breathe and assume that, like air, it flows into every house. But when you consciously look for the effect of the different kinds of daylight, or ask yourself why this or that room is pleasant and satisfying, then you know daylight as the force it is—one that creates moods, frames beauty, invites and repels, defines space, changes the color and shape of the things we see.

In the daylit house, natural light plays a feature role. It is a controlled element of design. In this house the designer plans from the start to capture the beauty, drama, warmth, and cheer that daylight has to offer.

One of the great advantages of the daylit house is the flexibility it gives the floor plan. In the conventional house, the arrangement of the rooms is restricted because every room has to get its daylight from an outside wall. The light that's most typical of the daylit house comes in from overhead. This allows you to put rooms wherever you want them, and give them all the natural light they need simply by the use of a skylight, clerestory windows, or possibly a window wall.

The principles of the daylit house are valid anywhere, but the applications vary with the tremendous differences among climates. To use daylight effectively, the designer has to know a good deal about his climate, the changing quality of daylight from season to season, and the characteristics of the light from each compass direction.

Why Have a Skylight?

A skylight's primary function, of course, is simply to bring in natural light from overhead. But the specific effect it has on the room it lights, and the experience it offers people who are in or passing through the room can be very pleasant and exciting.

At one end of the range of uses is the skylight in a work area where you want all the glare-free light you can get. At the other extreme is the one that suffuses a wall with soft, natural light, or that gently illuminates a piece of sculpture in a hall or entry. Another candidate for attention is the entry. Here a skylight, or several of them, will raise the interior light level for a more gradual and pleasant transition from garden to house proper. Finally, the need for privacy can be an important factor. In a house on a narrow lot, for example, with windows facing a neighbor's house, you may have to draw the curtains even during the day. A skylight will eliminate the perpetual gloom. And, of course, putting artificial light in a skylight will even make it useful at night.

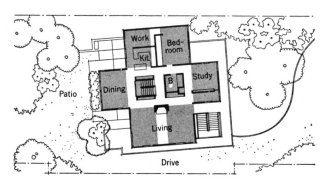

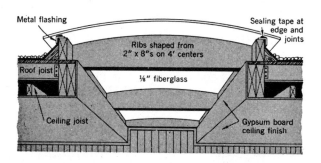

EVERY ROOM HAS SKYLIGHTING
Pictured on the cover, this house has glass walls that open it to out-of-doors and an unusual skylight system that opens the roof over every room. Unshaded portion of plan indicates skylights. Arch.: Jacob Robbins.

RUNS THE LENGTH OF A MAJOR ROOM
Wire glass skylight is low and unobtrusive from outside. Flat, plastic panels diffuse tube light on inside.

NATURAL LIGHT FOR BOOK-BROWSING
Hall and stairway benefit from skylight. There are no windows, but natural light from above is ample.

TRANSLUCENT ROOF ROLLS AWAY
An electrically operated plastic skylight gives the owners of this house a fingertip climate control for their patio. It's 13 feet wide, 20 feet long, and has a metal frame. Skylight design: Walter F. Vendetti.

(Continued on next page)

DAYLIGHT FOR CENTRAL HALL
Seven of eight skylights are visible in this view of an entry hall and corridor. Archs.: Bassetti and Morse.

A WINDOW IN THE ROOF
In wooded setting, a clear skylight opens this kitchen to the sky and the trees. Arch.: Ian Mackinlay & Assoc.

A WINDOWLESS ENTRY HALL
Skylights brighten this entry hall for pleasant transition from garden to house proper. Arch.: Germano Milono.

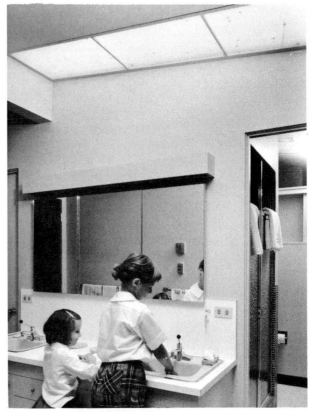

PANEL SKYLIGHTS FOR BATHROOM
Panel skylights in interior bathroom, hall outside, diminish sense of confinement. Archs.: Bassetti and Morse.

The Benefits of Clerestory Windows

Whereas a skylight generally is an opening in a roof (flat or pitched), a clerestory is a vertical opening in a wall plane that goes above the normal ceiling height. Both skylights and clerestories can be made to open or be of fixed construction.

In many ways the clerestory window gives the best demonstration of the benefits of daylighting from high overhead. Clerestory windows almost always require a lofty ceiling, usually a change in ceiling level, and therefore tend to create interesting variety of interior spaces. Clerestory windows allow you to see upward and out; indeed they tend to lead your eye out of its accustomed horizontal path to explore upward. Also, clerestory lighting usually entails fewer direct sun problems than skylights; windows can be sheltered under a roof overhang, or the direct sun confined to a comparatively small aperture.

Finally, clerestory lighting demonstrates one of the most pleasant aspects of daylighting from high overhead by providing change and multiplicity in the light by which you see objects.

GLASS FOR VIEWS, LIGHT, COLOR
Clerestory above living room (above left) has colorful stained glass panels on street side. Window seats (above right) are for view-watching. Chimney visible through clerestory. Arch.: Daniel M. Streissguth.

HIGH GLASS PANELS ACT LIKE CLERESTORY
In house with standard-height ceiling, high glass panels light stairwell, create vertical space. Arch.: Henrik Bull.

CLERESTORY WINDOWS ALL AROUND
Clerestories light raised ceiling section of this living room and make it seem more lofty. Note treetop view.

(Continued on next page)

KITCHEN SOFTLY LIT FROM FOUR SIDES
Clerestory windows seem to elevate pyramidal ceiling, add to illusion of greater space. Archs.: Bassetti & Morse.

HIGH, CLERESTORY-LIT CEILING
Despite small size, high clerestories illuminate kitchen ceiling for spacious effect. Arch.: Fisk and Hodgkinson.

ROOF LINE PERMITS CLERESTORY LIGHTING FOR INTERIOR KITCHEN
Located in the center of the living zone (family room, dining area, kitchen, living room), this kitchen is well lighted by clerestory windows placed in the gabled roof line. Archs.: Criley and McDowell.

The Window Wall Two Stories High

Two-story glass dramatically opens both high-ceilinged living areas and interior balcony space to the outdoors, for effects far more interesting than a single-level ceiling allows. We've seen two-story window walls make a small house seem much larger, help fit a hillside house to its site and view, give a box-shaped house character inside and out, and open up a cabin to the grandeur of a mountain setting.

The problem of privacy is less in a house on a hillside or in dense woods, than in the usual city house. Several ways to achieve privacy from the street are simply to place the carport in front of the house, extend high side walls toward the street, or use two-story draperies. Indoors, the farther the upstairs balcony is from the window wall, the more likely the need for a low balcony wall or cabinets as a privacy screen. You may need only a protective open railing where the balcony is close to the glass.

Sun control is often another problem but most home owners with window walls tend to feel that the benefits overbalance any discomfort that might be experienced from the sun. The sun can be controlled with draperies or blinds in most cases, or with some of the devices used for privacy. For further ideas, see pages 118-121.

GLASS WALL LIGHTS TERRACE AND MAIN FLOORS
Floor extends out through a glass wall to become terrace; the sun brightens both. Arch.: Robert Green.

WINDOW WALL OPENS TO SKY AND VIEW
Balcony gives sheltering effect in pleasant contrast to freedom of open space beyond. Archs.: Marquis & Stoller.

TWO-STORY GLASS FOR INTERIOR COURT
On narrow lot, glass wall contributes to apparent size of court. Archs.: Killingsworth, Brady, Smith & Assoc.

Some imaginative ways of using artificial light

Just as a fresh coat of paint can rescue a house from drabness, the right kind of lighting can enliven a house after dark, create a mood, and even produce a kind of enchantment on long winter nights.

All the different lighting ideas shown on these pages are architectural; that is, each solution is designed to be built in as a permanent part of the room. They reflect a continuing search by home owners and those who are in the planning stages for a new home for individual answers to specific problems, often with professional help in design. Although in some cases manufactured fixtures could have been used, these solutions have the special interest of "one-of-a-kind" answers.

The results of this search make up a kind of catalog of lighting devices. Broad-source lighting is one category; a low-brightness source lights a wide area. Other classical devices are down-light, in which the area is extended by the use of a number of small light sources; multiple panels; the cove; the valance; the luminous ceiling; a variation of the valance; and the soffit.

In all of these the light source is shielded from view from the side. In most of them a diffuser—a panel of translucent glass or plastic or a grille—shields the source of light and also diffuses light to the side. Most of the other individual lights in this collection are also shielded and diffused.

SIX DOWN-LIGHTS IN DROPPED CEILING
Six low-voltage (6-volt) down-lights illuminate the entire alcove with overlapping light patterns. They are a set of garden lights, held by redwood brackets screwed to gypsum board ceiling; switch behind curtain.

WOODEN GRILLES FOR RECESSED FIXTURES
Handsome with wood interior, grilles cover recessed fixtures inside house as well as soffit lights outside.

TUBE LIGHTING AUGMENTS LIGHT FROM LAMP
Tube lighting on top of bookcase bounces light off ceiling; source shielded by fascia. Arch.: Vladimir Ossipoff.

LIGHT PATTERN ON DRAPERIES
Clear bulbs in ceiling fixtures cast interesting pattern on draperies; chandelier adds to effect. Design: John Kapel.

FLUORESCENT TUBES BEHIND VALANCE
Living room has no separate lamps, just fluorescent tubes behind drapery valance with light shining up and down.

(Continued on next page)

SUNNY PHOTOGRAPH BRIGHTENS DARK HALL

Not open sky but a perpetually sunny photograph brightens formerly dark hall. Glass supports print in metal grille. Above photograph is a vented 3-foot enclosure which holds the four 150-watt reflector bulbs.

VALANCE OR COVE

This simple slanted shield directs light from bulbs upward, brightening room. Design: Norman V. Manoogian.

A CLEAR BULB AND OPEN FIXTURE

Fixture has wooden ring top and bottom with 24 wood slats; it uses a clear bulb. Archs.: Hart and Weiss.

DECORATIVE GLARE-REMOVING GRILLE
Simple wooden shields below ceiling level contain round bamboo trivets below bulbs. Design: John Kapel.

LIGHTING SOFFIT FOR CORNER OF ROOM
Lighting soffit above sofa has rigid translucent plastic panels, fluorescent tubes. Arch.: Fred Earl Norris.

FLUORESCENT TUBES FOR BATHROOM COUNTER
Over bathroom counter 40-watt fluorescent tubes give good working light; shower light is reflected in mirror.

LIGHTING PANEL FOR KITCHEN
Where wall meets ceiling, two double 4-foot fluorescent tube fixtures are mounted behind fiberglass-plastic panel.

HALL HAS LUMINOUS CEILING, LINEN CLOSET
Combination of luminous ceiling and a well lighted display area above linen closet make hallway seem larger.

PULL-OUT SHELF FOR SORTING LAUNDRY
A pull-out shelf in this hallway makes a handy spot for sorting laundry; stationary shelves hold books, magazines.

Adding interest to a narrow hallway

There's no questioning the fact that halls provide a necessary and efficient solution to the problem of getting people from one part of the house to another.

Unfortunately, they also are likely to be the most lifeless, uninteresting places in the whole house. On these pages we offer six sketches of ideas that could be applied in the planning or construction stages of a new house or incorporated in an existing house with minimum remodeling.

If you are handy with carpenter tools, there's no reason why you can't tackle any of the ideas illustrated here. But if your experience doesn't extend beyond putting up a towel rack, you'd better get some professional help from an alteration contractor or carpenter.

A REFERENCE LIBRARY
Books need more depth than wall thickness allows, so dictionary is on "fall-out bin rack" with counter balance.

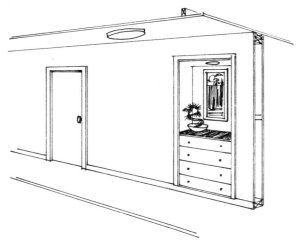

DISPLAY ALCOVE, STORAGE BELOW
Made from an old linen closet, this alcove has a series of drawers below. Door frame is finished with molding.

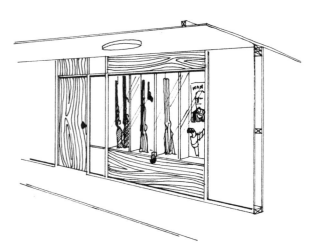

FOR GUN OR HOBBY COLLECTION
With glass doors you can lock, walls of hallway make good display case; wood panels replace gypsum board.

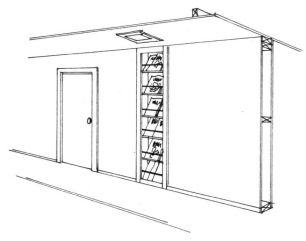

A MAGAZINE RACK
Magazine rack, illuminated by ceiling light, is only 13½ inches wide, can be inserted between existing studs.

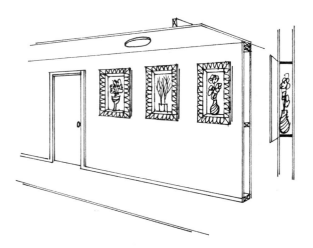

PICTURE FRAMES FOR VARIED OBJECTS
Picture frame molding sets off inserts between studs; can display dried arrangements, art objects, photographs.

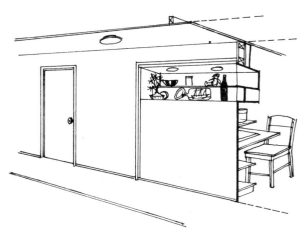

DISPLAY SHELVES
Double-faced case is set in opening between hall and adjoining room so display shelves can be seen from hall.

EXTERIOR DECKING EXTENDS LIVING ROOM
Inside, ¼-inch void between 2 by 3-inch members is filled with wood block set ½ inch below surface.

How to make a room seem larger

Small rooms can be made to appear larger by extending the material of the floor in an unbroken surface through a window wall to an outside living area and/or by the use of sliding glass doors that will open a room to the garden or a view.

Extending the material of the floor requires that you choose surfacing that will be compatible indoors yet rugged and durable to withstand variable weather conditions outdoors. In the living room (shown in the photograph above) and the bedroom (shown in the photograph at left below), the indoor-outdoor material is combined with carpeting that provides warmth and comfort. In the dining room (shown at right below), softness underfoot is not as necessary and the brick continues across the room and out through the window wall.

Installing sliding glass doors requires consideration of two factors. First, make certain that the wall to be opened is a bearing wall (any exterior or interior wall at right angles to the ceiling joists). Second, look at the wall from both sides; an opening centered in a wall may look all right from inside the room, but it may not be the most pleasant solution when you look at it from the outside.

RED BRICK LEADS TO SMALL COURTYARD
Red brick laid molded side up, extends from court through bedroom. Archs.: Schwager, Fernald, Ballew.

BRICK FLOOR CONTINUES THROUGH WINDOW WALL
Smooth brick on radiant heated subfloor extends through window wall to form patio. Archs.: Hester and Davis.

GLASS DOORS OPEN FAMILY ROOM TO DECK

Sliding glass doors open family room-dining area to generous-sized deck when additional space is needed for parties, dancing. Floor is uncarpeted; acoustical plaster ceiling controls sounds. Arch.: H. Douglas Byles.

A SEMI-OPEN LANAI

A sliding glass wall opens to a radiant heated lanai which has a canvas overhead and galvanized screening.

GLASS DOORS OPEN TO BEDROOM GARDEN

Indoor, outdoor areas are tied together through use of a glass wall and glass doors opening to private garden.

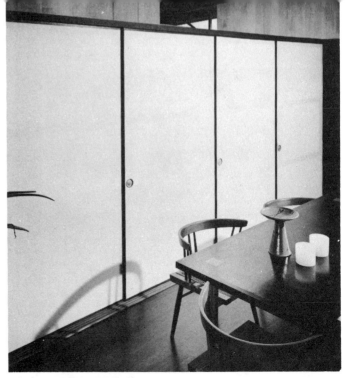

PANELS ARE COVERED IN UNBLEACHED MUSLIN
Covered panels operate on a floor guide and overhead tracks. Open, the four panels are telescoped. Closed, the panels conceal storage, screen kitchen area from formal dining area. Arch.: Thomas D. Perkins.

Screens are efficient...and give privacy

One way you can have privacy in an open plan house, and perhaps add to its efficiency, is to use fixed screens that act as "walls," but permit freer passage of light and air; or sliding panels so you can open up a large room or divide it into separate areas for various family activities.

In these photographs, we show some ways to use fixed and sliding screens. They're adaptable to many building situations: in a new home, for privacy within spacious rooms; in a remodeled home, to open up a wall but keep a sense of separation; in a small cabin, for privacy without splitting space into tiny rooms.

Translucent panels are valuable because they allow the passage of a diffused light. Sliding screens, of translucent or solid materials, usually operate on floor and overhead tracks. One or two sections may be fixed and the remaining panels then stack behind these; or the screen may retract entirely into a wall so it occupies no room space when out of use.

FIBERGLASS SET IN PLASTIC SLIDE
Two panels of fiberglass set in translucent plastic slide behind two fixed panels to open living area and family room to each other. Closed, these rooms are completely separated. Arch.: Paul Hayden Kirk.

DIVIDER SCREEN WITH OPEN PANELS
Plastic screen with open panels separates entry, dining area; is attached to wall. Design: Fred Hamack, Jr.

MOVABLE SHUTTERS AND SOLID PANEL
Solid panel (right) and movable shutters hung from ceiling close off area in open plan. Design: John Barkhorn.

OVERHEAD TRACK FOR SLIDING PANELS
Sliding panels mark off the living areas from hallway; permit free passage of light, air. Arch.: Paul Hayden Kirk.

INTERLOCKING PANELS PULL OUT OF WALL
Top-hung panels pull out of wall recess at right to make alcove into separate room. Arch.: Morgan Stedman.

(Continued on next page)

HUNG FROM TRACK BELOW PEAKED CEILING

A private dining area is created when four fiberglass and walnut panels are closed. The 8-foot-high overhead track is considerably lower than peaked ceiling, so air, sound can travel across top. Arch.: Robert Cooper.

TRANSLUCENT SCREEN PARTITIONS OFF HALLWAY

Striped wall was formerly a wall of kitchen; screen was installed to partition off hallway. End panels are fixed, two center sections glide on overhead track. Light easily passes through plastic. Design: Roy Krell.

PANELS OF BURLAP EMBEDDED IN PLASTIC WITH WALNUT FRAMES
Decorative even when pushed open along the wall, these panels do not stack one behind the other when open, but move on single track, remain in view; separate entry from dining room. Design: Virginia Anawalt.

SCREEN IS ACCORDION-FOLDED
Entry is screened from living area by simple wood frames inset with sheer rayon panels. Design: Albert E. Smith.

A FLOOR-TO-CEILING DIVIDER
Wood frame with fabric attached makes handsome divider; "ledge" holds small objects. Arch.: Burr Richards.

L-SHAPED ROOM WRAPS AROUND GARDEN

Lit by a glass skylight and ventilated by louvers in wall (background), this indoor garden brings a sense of intimacy with the land into corner of the house. Den is beyond. Archs.: Dennis, Slavsky & Whitaker.

Why not bring the garden indoors?

On these pages, we present six ideas on how you can include an indoor garden in your new home. Note the special charm you can give a house when you turn it inward to a garden. An interior garden can bring in sunshine, fresh air, good lighting, and a sense of intimacy with the land. If the delights are many, so are the practical aspects. For example, a garden built into a house can be the ideal solution for a subdivision house on a flat lot when people want privacy as well as openness and the benefits of a garden. It can be a garden to look at and it can be an all-year outdoor living area, protected from the wind. In winter, if it is enclosed (overhead or around the sides) it can act as a source of warmth. In summer heat, it can be a shady oasis; or if it is sunny, the warmed air will rise from it and draw cooler air from outer-wall windows through the house.

The advantages of a screened garden can be many: it can form a visual screen, especially between brightly lighted and darker areas; it can keep out wind-blown debris; it can form a barrier to keep in (or out) pets and small children; it can keep out insects (in areas with many flies or biting insects, this can often make the difference between being comfortable outdoors and staying inside); it can reduce glare and cut wind velocity.

As you will see from the six examples shown here, one of the simplest ways to include an interior garden is to use the space between two wings of the house; another effective way is to use an L formed by the house. You will also see how to get a similar effect by placing a garden outside a glass wall and enclosing it with a solid wall or fence farther out, and also some ways to let a garden penetrate through a house wall.

A four-room garden

House was planned so that its small and inviting garden could be entered from no less than four separate rooms — study, entry, living room, and master bedroom.

SCREENED GARDEN between house extensions has several rooms opening onto it. Folding doors of bedroom lead out to round stepping stones.

A screen will provide shelter

Walls of this garden are a redwood grille and a glass wall of the house. Overhead it can be open, screened, covered by an extension of an interior ceiling, or covered by reed matting.

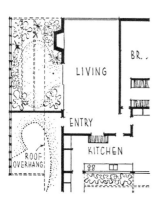

REDWOOD SCREEN gives privacy, sun, and wind protection to garden that opens beyond glass wall of living-dining room. Arch.: Josef van der Kar.

(Continued on next page)

This garden
has reed overhead

The floor plan below shows how wall of the house extends just a short distance out to enclose the garden. A reed screen overhead protects garden from sun, casts pleasing pattern of sun and shade on the house walls.

NO DRAPERIES *for privacy, sun control are needed on glass wall facing garden; exterior wall of house used in background. Arch.: Henry H. Hester.*

Garden that's
entirely indoors

From the floor plan and photograph, you can see how this garden differs from others we show by not opening outdoors. However, its size, and the treatment of the walls around it almost as exterior walls, make it seem much more like an indoor extension of an outdoor garden than just an oversized indoor planter.

GARDEN IS SKYLIT *by translucent glass that continues outdoors scene (windows at right) inside the living room. Arch.: Earl Lehr Powell.*

Adjoining an open lanai

This garden, though under roof and a part of the indoors, also has a see-through screen which permits view of lanai. It helps to create a dramatic entry, and a glimpse of it is an interesting part of the view from the living room.

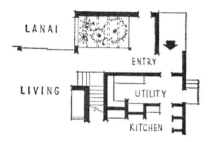

LATH AND WIRED GLASS overhead, screening, wall of hapu (tree fern bark) frame this fern and orchid garden. Arch.: Howard Cook.

A few container plants are sometimes enough

Master bedroom, dressing room, and the bathroom of this house work together as a unit in which the garden is an important part. From the outside, this small garden is carefully integrated with design of house exterior. A glass louver panel for ventilation is hidden behind curtain at the right.

BEDROOM AND ADJOINING BATHROOM share light and air of small, private deck enclosed with translucent glass panels. Arch.: Robert Grant.

A GIANT HORIZONTAL VENETIAN BLIND

Atrium patio has a positive sun control from this adjustable louver system. A metal arm attached to a cable operates louvers from below. Slats are hand-picked 1 by 6's, 16 feet long. Design: Weston L. Smith.

How to outwit the sun

All winter long we welcome the sun; then from about June through September we tax our ingenuity thinking up ways to control it. Shade is essential if we're to be comfortable during the summer. But how much and what kind of shade do you need to suit your requirements?

Although trees or patio overhead structures may solve the major problems, they don't always take care of requirements for spot or temporary shade—to screen out the afternoon sun at certain times of year, to give high noon shade for a dining table, to provide shade right now while trees are growing enough to take over the job.

When you need sun controls depends on where you live, how your house is sited, and how you've planned outdoor living areas. In cold-winter regions, for example, you may want to open the south side of your house to welcome the low winter sun. But in the desert, that low winter sun can be mighty bothersome. Any west-facing house near the Pacific Shore is apt to need some defense against the late afternoon sun in summer. And almost anywhere, the summer midday sun can make a patio uncomfortably hot and glaring.

Where the control is designed to keep the sun out of the house, you'll get less heat build-up inside if you can keep the glass or house siding from getting hot in the first place. Interior shades and draperies are effective sun blinds, but don't keep out much heat.

Here are several devices that may help you solve some specific shade problems.

FABRIC WINDOW SHADES

Handwoven reed and yarn used in shades control afternoon sun in this living room. Design: Hope Foote.

NO DRAPERIES ARE NEEDED

Woven blinds are fastened along eaves held taut by tent slides anchored to deck. Design: Harvey Ackerman.

SLAT SCREENS SHADE WINDOWS FROM SUN

Slats of 1 by 2's with 2 by 4-inch supports rest on concrete piers; tops are nailed to rafters. Screens can be painted or stained same color as house trim (or a harmonizing contrast). Design: Evald C. Moller.

(Continued on next page)

SLIDING SCREENS OF TINY LOUVERS
Sliding screens of tiny louvers outside living room reduce low winter sun glare and pool reflection. When not needed, screens stack four deep at either end of glass wall. Archs.: Benton and Park.

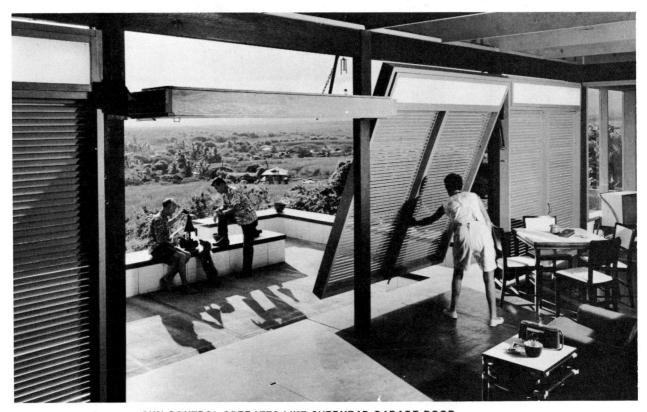

SUN CONTROL OPERATES LIKE OVERHEAD GARAGE DOOR
Each door, made of two panels of fixed wood louvers, pivots on 1-inch metal rod. Tension supplied by garage door springs. Lights at top operated by rheostat. Archs.: Lemmon, Freeth, Haines & Jones.

TRANSLUCENT PLASTIC DRAPERIES CONTROL GLARE

Custom-sized panels (multiples of 3-inch wide plastic strips hinged together) accordion-fold and stack to one side when not in use; 12-foot width reduces to just 1 foot. Panels control glare from patio and pool.

LOUVERED SHUTTERS THAT SLIDE

Visual effect and practicality of louvered shutters is retained despite lowered ceiling over remodeled break-fast area. Shutters on ceiling track move along guide at window sill (see right above).

Additional custom touches

On the following pages are additional ideas for enhancing the livability and personality of your home—whether you are planning your home, building it, or are already in it. Not every idea can be adapted exactly as shown for your own particular situation, but several of them may kindle your interest and help you put your own ingenuity to work.

This compilation represents only a sampling of custom touches from hundreds of homes that have been scouted and reported by the editors of *Sunset*. From a suspended ceiling that holds hi-fi speakers and light fixtures, to a see-through room divider on which cabinets and shelves can be hung—or even to the use of exposed aggregate concrete "carpeting" next to a fireplace—all of the ideas have been tested and tried by architects and homeowners.

OUT-OF-THE-WAY STAIRCASE
Circular stairway is recessed in exterior wall, takes little floor space from each floor. Arch.: Michel Marx.

A USEFUL SUSPENDED CEILING
Spaced 1 by 4's make trellis that hides hi-fi speakers and holds light fixtures; suspended by metal rods.

IT SLIDES OUTSIDE THE WALL
This glass door slides outside the wall (a door that slides into a wall often weakens it). The exposed unit is framed in 6 by 6-inch beams. Arch.: Morgan Stedman.

SLEEPING QUARTERS CONVERT TO PLAY AREAS
Room can be divided by folding wall pulled out from between built-in drawers. Folding doors separate it from sleep, play area (foreground). Arch.: Donald Goldman.

PASS-THROUGH TO OUTDOORS
Outdoor serving counter matches indoor center. Glass panel opens pass-through. Archs.: Smith and Williams.

PASS-THROUGH FACING THE VIEW
Dishes can go directly from table to sink and dishwasher. Countertop is a cement veneer. Arch.: Germano Milono.

FOR INTERIOR DOORWAYS
Draperies of dining room windows are carried on across the hall doorway—so extra panel can be drawn over opening at mealtime. Arch.: Morgan Stedman.

IT FOLDS TO THE WALL
Folding door works well in a tight space, folds against wall where its ash veneer matches wall paneling. Design: Superior Home Improvement Company, San Francisco.

(Continued on next page)

A BEDROOM DIVIDER
Open partition permits placement of bed and desk in the center of the room. Arch.: James K. Levorsen.

A SEE-THROUGH ROOM DIVIDER
Metal poles hold cabinets, shelves, and lights; divide living-dining room. Arch.: Martin Borenstein.

A FIREPLACE IN THE BEDROOM
This handsome ceramic fireplace provides heat as well as the pleasant sounds of a crackling fire. It rests on pebble-studded concrete base. Arch.: Van Evera Bailey.

LAVATORY FOR CHILDREN'S ROOM
Louvered doors open closet in bedroom to a large, well lighted mirror, a lavatory, and plenty of counter and drawer space. Archs.: Bakke-Cann-Page Associates.

LIGHT WITHOUT GLARE
Battens of board-and-batten siding extend up over glass to create grille; window is shaded by roof overhang.

KITCHEN WITHOUT CABINETS
For neatness, and to avoid high reaching, all storage is in drawers or on perforated hardboard on the walls.

A WOOD FLOOR IN THE KITCHEN
Protected by a synthetic resin finish, wood floor in kitchen is not as impractical as it sounds. Floor can be cleaned with damp mop. Arch.: Roland Terry and Assoc.

BUILD A TABLE AROUND A POST
This post supports a kitchen table three feet in diameter. Covered with laminated plastic, it's located at the traffic-free end of kitchen. Arch.: Richard Dennis.

(Continued on next page)

LIGHT, VIEW, VENTILATION
The two clear glass sections on either side of louvers are fixed, can be covered by curtains. Frosted louvers open for view and for ventilation. Arch.: Ernest H. Hara.

A PLYWOOD VENT
Plywood vent with screen (removed for the summer in this photo), beneath fixed glass panel permits air circulation, but doesn't impair view. Arch.: David Tucker.

THIS IS AGGREGATE "CARPETING"
Exposed-aggregate concrete was bonded to subfloor with concrete latex emulsion; aggregate used was pea gravel.

RETURN AIR GOES UNDER THE STEPS
Wood grilles in entryway steps are furnace's return-air openings, are out of the way. Arch.: Barry L. Wasserman.

ACOUSTICAL MATERIALS FOR OPEN AREAS UNDER CEILINGS

Light-colored, fissured acoustical tile reflects the cove lighting and absorbs the sound in this open living and dining area; draperies also help. Arch.: C. B. Alford.

Acoustical roof decking, usable where spacing between beams is 4 feet or less, is base for roofing on top; underside is ceiling surface. Design: William Gilman.

GENEROUS SPACE WITH LONG SPANNING STRUCTURES

Expressed in steel, post-and-beam form achieves long spans with lightness and rigidity. Archs.: Knorr & Elliott.

Glue-laminated wood beams make longer span than plain wood, can be formed in arches. Arch.: John J. Whelan.

PHOTOGRAPHERS

William Aplin: 34 (bottom), 56, 106, 119 (top right, bottom). Morley Baer: 15 (bottom), 24 (top), 40, 41, 109 (bottom right). Jeremiah O. Bragstad: 42. Ernest Braun: 7, 12, 13, 14, 16, 17, 20, 21, 23, 32, 33, 34 (top), 35, 59, 60, 61, 64, 65, 68, 69, 71, 72 (bottom), 73, 96, 100 (top), 103 (bottom left), 105 (top left), 123 (bottom right), 124 (top left), 125 (top right), 126 (top right), 127 (bottom left). Tom Burns, Jr.: 63. Camera Hawaii: 22. Clyde Childress: 54, 55, 109 (top). Glenn M. Christiansen: 11, 70, 72 (top right), 86, 87 (top left, middle, bottom), 90, 91, 95, 112 (bottom), 113 (bottom left), 126 (bottom left). Richard Dawson: 72 (top left). Dearborn-Massar: 10, 98 (top left, bottom right), 110 (bottom), 111 (bottom left), 113 (bottom right), 119 (top left). Max Eckert: 122 (bottom right). Amir Farr: 44 (bottom). Richard Fish: 57 (top), 58 (bottom), 66, 67, 76, 77, 78, 79, 80 (top), 94, 122 (top right), 123 (top left), 125 (top left). Frank L. Gaynor: 85, 88, 92, 93 (top left, top right). Vern Green: 101 (top left). Richard Gross: 44 (top). Bruce Harlow: 57 (bottom), 126 (bottom right). John Hartley: 25 (top), 93 (bottom), 108 (bottom left), 120 (top). Herrington-Olson Photography: 127 (top). Dean D. Hesketh Photography: 108 (top). Art Hupy: 111 (top left). Neil Koppes: 81, 82, 83, 87 (top left). Edmund Y. Lee: 37, 124 (bottom left). Jack McDowell: 43. Don Normark: 8, 9, 28, 29, 30, 31, 38, 39, 51, 84, 89, 99 (top), 112 (top), 125 (bottom left). Maynard L. Parker: 24 (bottom). Charles R. Pearson: 116 (bottom), 127 (bottom right). Photo Art: 104 (top). Photo Craft Co.-Hawaii: 19, 52, 53. Photographic Illustrators: 62. Gerald Ratto: 80 (bottom). Marvin Rand: 45, 50. Karl H. Riek: 15 (top). Martha Rosman: 98 (top right, bottom left), 113 (top), 122 (top left), 124 (top right, bottom right). Julius Shulman: 18, 26, 48, 49, 100 (bottom), 101 (right), 108 (bottom right), 115 (bottom). Douglas M. Simmonds: 46, 105 (top right), 116 (top), 117 (bottom). Hugh N. Stratford: 27, 36, 74, 75, 99 (bottom right). Mark Strizic & Ian B. McKenzie: 47. Darrow M. Watt: 97, 99 (bottom left), 102, 103 (top left, bottom right), 104 (bottom), 105 (bottom), 109 (bottom left), 111 (bottom right), 118, 121, 122 (bottom left), 123 (top right, bottom left). Al Weber: 58 (top). R. Wenkam: 25 (bottom), 103 (top right), 110 (top), 111 (top right), 114, 115 (top), 117 (top), 120 (bottom), 125 (bottom right), 126 (top left).